"This is the book that I was looking for v̱
tor of ministry program years ago! In this lucid and luminous treatment of
Christ's ministry to the Father on behalf of the world through the power of
the Holy Spirit, Stephen Seamands takes the doctrine of the Trinity off the
shelf and reveals the dynamic of God's mission of love and reconciliation
from the inside out. Combining scholarly insight with spiritual passion, Seamands traces out the contours of the divine mystery of redeeming love as
the image of that which all humans were created to be and that which we
who minister are called to do."

RAY S. ANDERSON, SENIOR PROFESSOR OF THEOLOGY AND MINISTRY, FULLER
THEOLOGICAL SEMINARY, AND AUTHOR OF THE SHAPE OF PRACTICAL THEOLOGY

"One of the quiet and unnoticed revolutions of our time has been the
extraordinary recovery of the doctrine of the Trinity in Christian circles.
Initially the crucial task was to come to terms historically, conceptually and
intellectually with this much-needed breakthrough. Yet the doctrine of the
Trinity was from the beginning not some abstract, numerical, metaphysical
dispute. The Trinity is the heartbeat of a life lived before God that cries out
for further exploration in the ministry of the church. Stephen Seamands has
answered that cry to telling effect. This is a work that is elegant, sensitive,
unpretentious, accessible and eminently practical. It displays a pleasing
familiarity with the critical literature; better still, it exhibits a burning piety
bereft of sentimentality and filled with realistic optimism. This is pastoral
theology at its very best!"

WILLIAM ABRAHAM, ALBERT COOK OUTLER PROFESSOR OF WESLEY STUDIES,
PERKINS SCHOOL OF THEOLOGY, SOUTHERN METHODIST UNIVERSITY, AND
AUTHOR OF THE LOGIC OF EVANGELISM

"Few wear the titles of theologian and pastor as well as Steve Seamands, pastoral theologian. Harvesting a bumper crop of contemporary reflection on
the triune nature of God, he is able to develop a theology of ministry that
flows from and mirrors the communal life of God: Father, Son and Spirit. At
once profound and disarmingly simple, here is the sort of theologically practical work that deserves a wide readership."

JOEL B. GREEN, VICE PRESIDENT OF ACADEMIC AFFAIRS AND PROVOST,
ASBURY THEOLOGICAL SEMINARY

"Truth about God is not merely academic. It's passionate and practical. Seamands's treatment of trinitarian theology did so much more than inform and challenge me. It did both, but it also reached my soul where the passion to enjoy their community and reveal their character burns like a hot fire."

LARRY CRABB, FOUNDER AND DIRECTOR, NEW WAY MINISTRIES

"One thing too often missing from the contemporary renaissance of the doctrine of the Trinity is its practical application, especially to ministry. Stephen Seamands has helpfully closed that gap with *Ministry in the Image of God*. Now we know how belief in the Trinity impacts the practices of ministry. Every Christian minister (lay or professional) interested in integrating theology with Christian service should read this book."

ROGER E. OLSON, PROFESSOR OF THEOLOGY, GEORGE W. TRUETT THEOLOGICAL SEMINARY, AND AUTHOR OF *THE STORY OF CHRISTIAN THEOLOGY*

"Seamands connects the dots between ancient doctrine, holy Scripture, modern theology and Christian experience, giving us a vision of the Trinity in life that is comprehensible, subtly childlike, a joy to embrace and an invitation to be embraced."

DAVID HANSEN, AUTHOR OF *THE ART OF PASTORING*, AND CONTRIBUTING EDITOR OF *LEADERSHIP JOURNAL*

"In a masterful way, Stephen Seamands teaches us afresh to think Trinity, own the mystery and live in the radical middle of God's mission. This book combines the power of old ideas and contemporary experience with life-changing outcome. I highly recommend it."

TIMOTHY C. MORGAN, DEPUTY MANAGING EDITOR, *CHRISTIANITY TODAY*

MINISTRY IN THE IMAGE OF GOD

The Trinitarian Shape
of Christian Service

STEPHEN SEAMANDS

An imprint of InterVarsity Press
Downers Grove, Illinois

InterVarsity Press
P.O. Box 1400, Downers Grove, IL 60515-1426
World Wide Web: www.ivpress.com
E-mail: mail@ivpress.com

InterVarsity Press® is the book-publishing division of InterVarsity Christian Fellowship/USA®, a student movement active on campus at hundreds of universities, colleges and schools of nursing in the United States of America, and a member movement of the International Fellowship of Evangelical Students. For information about local and regional activities, write Public Relations Dept., InterVarsity Christian Fellowship/USA, 6400 Schroeder Rd., P.O. Box 7895, Madison, WI 53707-7895, or visit the IVCF website at <www.intervarsity.org>.

Scripture quotations, unless otherwise noted, are from the New Revised Standard Version of the Bible, copyright 1989 by the Division of Christian Education of the National Council of the Churches of Christ in the USA. Used by permission. All rights reserved.

Design: Cindy Kiple

Images: Scala/Art Resource, NY

ISBN-10: 0-8308-3338-2
ISBN-13: 978-0-8308-3338-2

Printed in the United States of America ∞

Library of Congress Cataloging-in-Publication Data has been requested.

Seamands, Stephen A., 1949-
  Ministry in the image of God: the trinitarian shape of Christian
  service / Stephen Seamands.
      p. cm.
  Includes bibliographical references.
  ISBN 0-8308-3338-2 (pbk.: alk. paper)
  1. Pastoral theology. 2. Trinity. I. Title
  BV4011.3.S42 2006
  253—dc22
                                                          2005029024

P   19   18   17   16   15   14   13   12   11   10   9   8   7   6   5   4
Y   20   19   18   17   16   15   14   13   12   11   10   09

To my four adult children:

Matthew, Jason, Joseph and Stephanie.

What a joy and blessing you are to me!

"I will pour out my Spirit on your offspring,

and my blessing on your descendants.

They will spring up like grass in a meadow,

like poplar trees by flowing streams.

One will say, 'I belong to the LORD';

another will call himself by the name of Jacob;

still another will write on his hand, 'the LORD's,'

and will take the name Israel."

ISAIAH 44:3-5 (NIV)

CONTENTS

TRINITARIAN MINISTRY

Why It Matters

I bind unto myself the name,
the strong name of the Trinity,
by invocation of the same,
the Three in One, the One in Three,
of whom all nature has creation:
eternal Father, Spirit, Word.
Praise to the Lord of my salvation!
Salvation is of Christ the Lord. Amen.

PATRICK OF IRELAND

❖

Bill's face wore a baffled expression. He was a seasoned pastor, enrolled in my theology of ministry class in our doctor of ministry program. I had begun the first session stressing the importance of theological foundations for ministry practice. "We need to know the 'why-tos' of ministry as well as the 'how-tos,'" I remarked. Everyone seemed to nod in agreement.

"All right," I continued, "let's consider the following description of Christian ministry: The ministry we have entered is the ministry *of*

Jesus Christ, the Son, *to* the Father, *through* the Holy Spirit, for the sake of the church and the world."

This description, quite foreign to Bill's pragmatic way of thinking, evoked his puzzled look. It was particularly the trinitarian focus of the description that perplexed him. Of course he affirmed the doctrine of the Trinity, but like many Christian leaders, although he gave lip service to the doctrine, he had never considered it relevant to the vocation of ministry. Such an explicitly trinitarian description of ministry took him by surprise.

According to Roderick Leupp, many Christians view the Trinity as "a riddle wrapped up inside a puzzle and buried in an enigma."[1] It's a riddle—how can something be one and three?—a puzzle since it seems irrational, and an enigma because even if you understood it, what practical value does it have? Better then to "leave well enough alone" and accept it by faith. Let theologians worry about it, but don't think about it yourself.

Unfortunately, most of us pastors and Christian leaders haven't advanced much beyond this either. In Bible school, college or seminary, we may have studied the historical development of the doctrine of the Trinity, grasped the connection between the Trinity and the Christian view of salvation, and become familiar with trinitarian heresies such as modalism and tritheism. In our ministerial practice, we baptize persons in the trinitarian name of God. During worship, we sing the doxology, praising Father, Son and Holy Spirit, or hymns like "Holy, Holy, Holy" extolling "God in three persons, blessed Trinity!" We pronounce the benediction using the words of 2 Corinthians 13:14: "The grace of the Lord Jesus Christ, the love of God, and the communion of the Holy Spirit be with all of you."

But aside from such occasional references, our thoughts about the Trinity are few and far between. In the daily grind of ministry, no

Christian doctrine seems more far removed and less practically relevant. The notion that the Trinity might provide a foundation and framework for our vocation rarely enters our mind.

That is why I have written this book—to demonstrate the significance of the doctrine of the Trinity for the vocation of ministry. Having spent eleven years as a local church pastor and more than twenty years as a seminary professor of theology who equips persons preparing for Christian service, I am convinced that no doctrine is, in fact, more relevant to our identity and calling as ministers than the Trinity. Many view the Trinity as a problem, difficult to understand and explain. At first glance it may appear that way, but as we ponder it, we find the opposite is true. The Trinity is a solution that makes so many perplexing issues intelligible.

The doctrine of the Trinity has been described as the grammar of the Christian faith. A grammar is a set of rules governing a particular language. It tells us how to speak the language correctly and to properly convey our meaning. As the Christian grammar, trinitarian doctrine enables us to speak rightly about the God who is revealed in Scripture as Father, Son and Holy Spirit. In fact, it is this doctrine that makes the Christian understanding of God distinctly Christian and not merely theistic.

Of course, one may understand and speak a language without knowing its grammar. Grammar itself doesn't convey meaning and content, except about the language itself. Often committed Christians can't articulate an understanding of the Trinity, yet they grasp it intuitively. Nevertheless, as is the case with any language, knowledge of trinitarian grammar is important. Without it we can't fathom the richness or depth of the Christian understanding of God, nor can we communicate it effectively to others. Therefore it's crucial for Christian leaders to know the rules of trinitarian grammar.

ENTERING INTO THE LIFE OF THE TRINITY

However, the primary purpose of the trinitarian grammar is not comprehension or communication, but communion with God. It shapes our language about God to shape our heart so we might share in the life of God. So Jesus intercedes for his future disciples: "As you, Father, are in me and I am in you, *may they also be in us*" (John 17:21, italics mine). The trinitarian circle of Father, Son and Holy Spirit is therefore an open, not a closed, circle. Through faith in Christ, through baptism *into* the name of the Father, Son and Holy Spirit (Matthew 28:19), we enter into the life of the Trinity and are graciously included as partners.

Someday what Jesus prayed for and what we already know now in part will be known in full. At the consummation there will be, as John Wesley describes it, "a deep, an intimate, an uninterrupted union with God; a constant communion with the Father and his Son Jesus Christ, through the Spirit; a continual enjoyment of the Three-One God, and of all creatures in him."[2] Such is God's desire for us, that we become, as the apostle Peter says, "participants of the divine nature." (2 Peter 1:4). Of course, this participation doesn't mean that our personal identity is lost in God or that our human nature actually becomes divine. God dwells in us and we dwell in God, but our radical divine-human differences are never blurred, nor do we ever merge with one another. Yet what a rich, joyous union with the triune God is offered to us.

The *Icon of the Holy Trinity*, painted in 1425 by Andrei Rublev, a Russian monk, powerfully conveys God's intention. Based on the story in Genesis 18, on one level the icon depicts the three angelic visitors who ate the meal Abraham and Sarah offered them and announced to the elderly couple the unexpected birth of their son, Isaac. But on another level, the three angels sitting around the table represent the three persons of the holy Trinity.[3]

Icon of the Holy Trinity

Although their heads are tilted at different angles toward one another, their faces are identical, and each holds a staff, suggesting they equally possess divine authority. Each of the figures wears a blue robe, again pointing to their oneness of being, yet they also wear different-colored garments, indicating their distinctive identities. Their faces, bent toward each other, disclose their humble, self-effacing love for one other, while their gleaming eyes convey their enjoyment. No one is speaking, but an intimate conversation is going on.

The central focus of the icon—what their conversation seems to be about—is the lamb contained in a chalice sitting on the center of the table. As Henri Nouwen suggests, here it "becomes the sacrificial lamb, chosen by God before the creation of the world, led to be slaughtered on Calvary and declared worthy to break the seven seals of the scroll."[4] In distinct ways, the hands of the three figures reveal the lamb's significance. The hand of the Son, represented by the middle figure, points with two fingers directly at the lamb in the chalice, acknowledging his mission of being "the Lamb of God who takes away the sin of the world" (John 1:29). The hand of the Father, the figure on the left, is raised in blessing over the chalice, thus encouraging the Son in his work. The hand of the Spirit, the figure on the right, is pointed to a rectangular opening in front of the table, signifying the world. The Son comes and offers himself for the world, and through the Spirit the world is brought to the Son and the Father.

Rublev's icon thus profoundly conveys the nature of the Trinity. If ever a picture was worth a thousand words, this one certainly is. As a theology professor in this visually oriented age, I have found it extremely helpful in presenting the doctrine of the Trinity to my students.

But Rublev has a deeper purpose for his icon than teaching doctrine. He wants it to effect communion with God, not merely communication of truth. As we contemplate it, says Nouwen, "we come to experience a gentle invitation to participate in the intimate conversation that is taking place among the three divine angels and to join them around the table. The movement from the Father toward the Son and the movement of both Son and Spirit toward the Father becomes a movement in which the one who prays is lifted up and held secure."[5] Rublev's icon beckons us to enter the circle of love, the divine life of the blessed Trinity. That is its ultimate purpose.

And that too is the ultimate purpose of the doctrine of the Trinity. It tells us not only about the nature of God but, as Catherine Mowry LaCugna says, about "God's life with us and our life with each other."[6] The One in whom we live and move and have our being (Acts 17:28) lives and moves and has his being as Father, Son and Holy Spirit. Divine revelation and redemption reflect God's trinitarian nature. Our experience of God in salvation and our life together as the church in worship, fellowship and mission are trinitarian as well. Indeed, in all his dealings and interactions with us—personal, corporate, social, cosmic—God goes the way of his trinitarian being.

The same holds true for the focus of this book, the vocation of ministry. It too will reflect the trinitarian pattern. Without it, Christian ministry becomes another helping profession and Christian service is a generic form of caregiving. Hence the description I offered to the class: The ministry into which we have entered is the ministry *of* Jesus Christ, the Son, *to* the Father, *through* the Holy Spirit, for the sake of the church and the world.

THE TRINITARIAN RENAISSANCE

Later in this chapter I will unpack that description, but first I want to place the trinitarian shape of ministry in a broader context by considering it in light of the current resurgence of interest among theologians in the doctrine of the Trinity.

To grasp the significance of this revival of trinitarian theology, we must go back to the eighteenth-century Enlightenment, when outspoken critics of the doctrine put orthodox Christians on the defensive. Philosophers like Immanuel Kant declared, "The doctrine of the Trinity provides nothing, absolutely nothing of practical value, even if one claims to understand it; still less when one is convinced that it far surpasses our understanding."[7] Reflecting the antitrinitarian spirit of the times, Thomas Jefferson became a Unitarian. Belief in the Trinity, he insisted, was mathematical nonsense.

In attempting to reach out to such "cultured despisers" of the Christian faith who believed the Trinity was untenable on rational and practical grounds, nineteenth-century theologians like Friedrich Schleiermacher significantly downplayed the Trinity. In *The Christian Faith,* his creative and extremely influential systematic theology published in 1830, Schleiermacher relegated discussion of the Trinity to the final chapter. He believed it was a doctrine of secondary importance and could be jettisoned with no essential loss. Although there were exceptions, for the next hundred years, theologians, following Schleiermacher's lead, politely retreated from the doctrine.

In the early decades of the twentieth century, however, that retreat came to an abrupt halt. Flying in the face of what he believed was Schleiermacher's wrongheaded approach to theology, Karl Barth placed the Trinity at the very beginning of his *Church Dogmatics* (1932). "The doctrine of the Trinity," he insisted, "is what basically distinguishes the Christian doctrine of God as Christian, and therefore what already distinguishes the Christian concept of revelation as Christian, in contrast to all other possible doctrines of God or concepts of revelation."[8]

By convincingly demonstrating the centrality of the Trinity in Christian theology, Barth paved the way for the resurgence of interest in the doctrine during the rest of the twentieth century and continuing today. Following Barth, Protestant theologians such as Jürgen Moltmann, Wolfhart Pannenberg and Eberhard Jüngel in Germany; T. F. Torrance and Colin Gunton in the United Kingdom; Ted Peters, Miroslav Volf, Elizabeth Johnson, Robert Jenson and Millard Erickson in North America; Leonardo Boff, Okechukwu Ogbonnaya and Jung Young Lee in Latin America, Africa and Asia have all written significant works on the Trinity. Hans Urs von Balthasar and Karl Rahner led the way in reviving interest in the Trinity among Roman Catholics and have been followed by Catherine Mowry LaCugna and Walter Kasper. Among Orthodox theologians, Vladimir Lossky and John Zizoulas have also made substantial contributions to the trinitarian renaissance.

Indeed, as the twenty-first century approached, theologians were publishing so many books and articles about the Trinity that David Cunningham described the phenomenon as "not so much like a renaissance as a bandwagon." Unlike the nineteenth century, when it was threatened by obscurity caused by neglect, now, he suggested, the doctrine of the Trinity "seems more likely to be obscured by an overabundance of theologians clustered around it."[9]

THE TRINITY AND THE VOCATION OF MINISTRY

As a professor who teaches theology, I have been able to read much of the literature contributing to the current trinitarian renaissance and have been greatly enriched by it. But as one who considers himself, first and foremost, a pastoral and practical theologian, I am concerned that many Christian leaders remain unaware that a trinitarian renaissance has been going on.

I think I understand why. Many of the significant theological works on the Trinity are simply too dense and abstract to be accessible to the average pastor or person in ministry. The writings of theologians are often so theoretical in nature they seem irrelevant to those engaged in the day-to-day practice of ministry, so practitioners shy away from them. As a result, when they reflect theologically on their ministerial practice, they do so with very little reference to the doctrine of the Trinity.

My concern is to help them do that. Several years ago when Martin Marty, a prolific author and astute observer of the North American religious scene, was lecturing on our campus, I attended a luncheon with him. When a member of our faculty asked him about the kind of Christian books needed today, he responded, "So many Christian books written today are either 'theologically theological' or 'practically practical.' What we need most are books that are 'theologically practical.'" That's my goal in writing this one. In considering the trinitarian shape of ministry, I want to be theologically practical.

As I've studied Scripture, Christian history and current literature on the Trinity, I have discerned seven characteristics of trinitarian life that have profound implications for the vocation of ministry. These seven characteristics delineate the nature of the trinitarian fellowship, the "life together" of Father, Son and Holy Spirit. They tell us how the Three-in-One God "lives and moves and has his being." And since we have entered this triune fellowship, they describe how we ought to "live and move and have our being" too. Each characteristic is significant for understanding the Christian life and ministry and for constructing a Christian worldview.

I will devote a chapter to each characteristic. To give you an idea where we are headed, here are my seven chapter titles, which explore these characteristics and suggest their relation to an understanding of ministry shaped by the Trinity:

• Relational Personhood: The Nature of Trinitarian Ministry

- Joyful Intimacy: The Foundation of Trinitarian Ministry
- Glad Surrender: The Heart of Trinitarian Ministry
- Complex Simplicity: The Mystery of Trinitarian Ministry
- Gracious Self-Acceptance: The Particularity of Trinitarian Ministry
- Mutual Indwelling: The Reciprocity of Trinitarian Ministry
- Passionate Mission: The Impulse of Trinitarian Ministry

As you read through this list, you may be wondering, *What in the world does that mean?* In the following chapters, as we explore each characteristic, I am confident that its meaning will become perfectly clear—perhaps even painfully clear. For conforming ourselves and our ministries to them will certainly involve change.

Again, the doctrine of the Trinity is the grammar of Christian faith and life. Like grammatical rules, these seven characteristics ought to become working principles in our ministries. They have profound implications for preaching, care giving, leading, teaching, administrating, praying and evangelizing. You can apply them to planning worship, directing a staff, counseling, discipleship, working with children or youth, resolving congregational conflicts, spiritual formation, planting a church or ministering crossculturally. I pray that as a result of reading this book, you will begin using these seven characteristics as a grid for evaluating your ministry. For the more you learn to "think Trinity" and live out these characteristics, the richer and more fruitful your ministry will become, since it will conform to the trinitarian image of God.

In relating these seven characteristics of trinitarian life to the vocation of ministry, I will apply them more to the *life* of ministry than the *work* of ministry. Three times in his conversation with Peter when he was reinstating him following his threefold denial, the risen Christ

asked him a question, "Do you love me?" which was then followed
by a command, "Feed my sheep" (John 21:15-17). The question focused on Peter's *relationship with* Christ; the command focused on his
work for Christ. Of course, the vocation of ministry includes both,
and the two are inextricably bound up together. Moreover, the seven
characteristics apply to both. However, in the chapters that follow, I
will concentrate more on the first (who we are in Christ) than the second (what we do for Christ). My main concern, in fact, is to apply
the characteristics to the spiritual life of the minister.

But before we embark on that journey, let's consider, one at a time,
the trinitarian phrases in the description of ministry introduced at
the beginning of this chapter: The ministry we have entered is the
ministry *of* Jesus Christ, *to* the Father, *through* the Holy Spirit, for the
sake of the church and the world.

THE MINISTRY *OF* JESUS CHRIST

In the daily grind of ministry it's easy to forget whose ministry it is.
Although we desire to serve Christ and often ask him for help, we assume that it's our ministry and we are the principal actors. This common understanding of ministry is partially true, but the profounder
truth is that the ministry we have entered is, first and foremost, the
ministry of Jesus Christ. It's his ministry more than ours.

Ministry, then, is not so much asking Christ to join us in our ministry as we offer him to others; ministry is participating with Christ
in his ongoing ministry as he offers himself to others through us.

Luke conveys this Christ-centered understanding of ministry at
the very beginning of the book of Acts. In Luke's first book (the
Gospel of Luke), as he reminds Theophilus, he recounted "all that
Jesus *began to do and to teach*" (Acts 1:1 NIV). By using the imperfect
Greek verb tense (signifying ongoing action, *began to do and to*

teach) rather than the aorist tense (signifying completed action, *did and taught*), Luke implies that Christ's earthly ministry didn't end with his death, resurrection and ascension to God's right hand. That's why he is writing a second book (Acts)—to tell the story of the ongoing ministry of Jesus through his apostles. As biblical expositor John Stott explains,

> Luke's first two verses are, therefore, extremely significant. It is no exaggeration to say that they set Christianity apart from all other religions. These regard their founder as having completed his ministry during his lifetime. Luke says Jesus only began his. . . . For after his resurrection, ascension, and gift of the Spirit, he continued his work, first and foremost through the unique foundation ministry of his chosen apostles and subsequently through the post-apostolic church of every period and place.[10]

Jesus' earthly ministry, therefore, didn't end when he returned to his Father in heaven. Through his body, the church, it merely assumed a different shape. The ministry we have entered is meant to be an extension of his. In fact, all authentic Christian ministry participates in Christ's ongoing ministry. Ministry is essentially about our joining Christ in his ministry, not his joining us in ours.

So much of our stress and burnout is the direct result of our failure to grasp this basic truth about ministry. We are carrying burdens that we were never designed to carry—burdens that Christ never intended for us to carry. Instead of following Christ the Leader, we wrongly assume the burden of leadership ourselves. No wonder we collapse under its weight.

Understanding *whose* ministry it is can be tremendously liberating. Jesus' words "My yoke is easy, and my burden is light" (Matthew

11:30) apply to ministry too! Granted, the yoke of ministry is often heavy, but realizing it is *Christ's* yoke and *Christ's* ministry causes the weight to shift. He carries the burden more than we do. Despite all the demands and pressures, we experience freedom, rest and joy, knowing that the outcome ultimately depends on Christ, not on us.

However, most of us find it difficult to live according to this truth. We are often tempted to take the burden of ministry on ourselves. A few years ago I had accepted an invitation to speak and lead workshops at a large Christian conference. As I was preparing my message for one of the plenary sessions, I became increasingly worried and anxious. Most of the people attending this conference were a part of a denominational circle I rarely moved in. Knowing that made me very unsure of myself. *What if I say something inappropriate? What if I'm not on the same wavelength they are?* Questions like these began to weigh heavily on me. Soon I was imagining all sorts of worst-case scenarios.

After several days of fretting, I got up one morning to pray. At the time I was engaged in a verse-by-verse devotional study of the Song of Solomon.[11] That particular morning I was meditating on verse 2:8: "The voice of my beloved! / Look, he comes, / leaping upon the mountains, / bounding over the hills."

Mountains and hills in Scripture often represent obstacles that confront us. That day my obstacle was the sermon I had to prepare for the conference. As I meditated on this verse, Jesus, my beloved, spoke to me: "Steve, why are you so uptight? This is so easy for me. It may seem like a mountain to you, but it's a molehill to me! I can leap and bound over it effortlessly. I have a sermon I want to preach to the people who will be gathered there. I'm going to preach it through you. In fact it's going to be fun! Come on, let's run together."

In that moment I realized what I had been doing. "Forgive me, Lord," I prayed, "Forgive me for taking this burden upon myself. I've made this all about me and my preaching performance. It's more about you than it is about me. Help yourself to me, Lord. Use me to accomplish your ministry. I want to run with you."

Later that day as I worked on the message, the dark cloud of worry that had been hanging over me evaporated, and the burden lifted. My heart was filled with joy and anticipation, and I no longer dreaded the preparation. What before had been drudgery actually turned to delight! Jesus was leading now, and I was following. On the day I preached at the conference, I was relaxed and confident. Instead of trying to get Christ to bless my ministry, I was blessed as I joined him in his.

The ministry we have entered is first and foremost the ministry *of Jesus Christ.* We must never forget that! Describing the nature of pastoral ministry, Thomas Oden sums up what is true of all forms of ministry: "The working minister is in a co-working ministry day after day with Christ's own ministry. . . . This is the centerpiece of care of souls: Jesus the overshepherd of our shepherding. . . . It is not what the pastor is out there doing that counts, but what Christ is doing through the pastor."[12]

TO THE FATHER

If the ministry we have entered is the ministry of Jesus Christ, then like his, ours will be directed primarily to the Father, not to the needs or demands of those around us.

Consider, for example, Jesus' healing of the man at the pool of Bethesda. Although many invalids—blind, lame and paralyzed—were there who needed healing (John 5:2), Jesus restored only one man that day. If he had let human need dictate his agenda, surely he would have healed many more. On the other hand, if the religious leaders had had their way, he would have healed no one because it was the sabbath. Why, then, did he heal on the sabbath, and why only one person? In answering his critics, Jesus explained: "My Father is still working, and I also am working. . . . Very truly, I tell you, the Son can do nothing on his own, but only what he sees the Father doing; for whatever the Father does, the Son does likewise" (John 5:17, 19).[13]

Ray Anderson shows how Jesus' actions follow a similar pattern in the story of the raising of Lazarus. Because of their brother's critical condition, Mary and Martha, the sisters of Lazarus, send Jesus a message: "Lord, he whom you love is ill" (John 11:3). By calling Lazarus "he whom you love," their message is designed to make Jesus feel obligated so he will come quickly.

But Jesus *doesn't* rush to Lazarus' side. After he receives the message, he stays "two days longer in the place where he was" (John 11:6). Consequently, when Jesus does finally arrive on the scene, in Mary and Martha's eyes he is four days too late. Lazarus is dead and buried. And when the sisters individually speak to Jesus, they both let him know they are disappointed in him: "Lord, if you had been here, my brother would not have died" (John 11:21, 32). Reflecting on Jesus' deliberate delay, Anderson observes, "This much is clear. The love of Jesus for Lazarus and the desperate plea of the two sisters did not set the agenda for the ministry of Jesus. This need from the side of the world did not take precedence over his commitment to serve the Father."[14]

Later when Jesus stands at Lazarus' tomb, he demands that the stone be removed. Now it's Mary and Martha's turn to delay. "Lord," they protest, "Why do that now? It's too late. His body is decomposing. There will be a terrible stench!" Earlier they tried to get Jesus to act; now they don't want him to! But Jesus insists, so they take away the stone. And then he raises Lazarus from the dead.

Of course, Jesus often met human needs and requests, but this story demonstrates that they did not dictate the direction of his ministry; his ministry to the Father did. As Anderson maintains, "The ministry of Jesus to the Father on behalf of the world is the inner logic of all ministry. Every aspect of the ministry of Jesus is grounded in the inner relation of mutual love and care between the Father and the Son. . . . His ministry is first of all directed to God and not to the world. The needs of the world are recognized and brought into this ministry but do not set the agenda."[15]

Unfortunately for many of us today, the church and the world, not the Father, are setting our agenda in ministry. Instead of being directed primarily to the Father for the sake of the church and the world, our ministry is directed primarily to the church and the world for the sake of the Father. The difference is subtle yet sublime and has profound implications for our life and work.

For one thing, it underscores the importance of our love relationship with the Father. Above I cited John 5:19, where Jesus says that he only does what he sees the Father doing. Notice what he says next: "The Father *loves* the Son and *shows* him all that he himself is doing" (John 5:20). There is a close connection between the love of the Father and the revelation of his will. Out of the Father and Son's relation of mutual love for one another, Christ's ministry flows. The same ought to hold true for us.

Oswald Chambers maintains that we "slander God by our very eagerness to work for Him without knowing Him."[16] That is always a temptation in ministry—to want to do things *for* God without cultivating our relationship *with* God. More about this in chapter three, where we will consider the intimate love of the Father, Son and Holy Spirit for one another and for us as the foundation out of which ministry should flow.

A Father-directed understanding of ministry also underscores the importance of learning to discern what the Father is doing. We often get in front of God by the multiplicity of our own works. The enormous needs of the church and the world cry out for our attention. Yet involvement in these good things can keep us from the best—the particular things the Father is doing that he wants us to be doing. Sometimes we can miss God's work by our very desire to do God's will!

Confronted by a sea of human need and the insatiable demands of people, those in ministry can become, in Stanley Hauerwas's phrase, "a quivering mass of availability." In earnestly seeking to do God's will, we can be tempted to do too much of it. In his spiritual counsel to a group of nuns, John of the Cross wisely cautions, "Without the command of obedience, you never take upon yourself any work—apart from the obligations of your state—however good and full of charity it may seem."[17] He recognizes that there is a profound difference between doing things for God and doing what God tells us to do.

Of course we must not overspiritualize or mystify the process of discerning what the Father is doing. As in the ministry of Jesus, the Father shows us what he wants us to do not mainly through mystical illuminations but in the context of the circumstances and events unfolding around us. Those who have reflected deeply on divine guidance stress that discerning God's will happens in a variety of ways, some which are very "natural" and others more "supernatural."[18] We should not set them against each other, nor elevate some as more spiritual than others, but use them all to determine what we should do in the light of what the Father is doing.

THROUGH THE HOLY SPIRIT

Discerning the Father's will leads us to the indispensable role of the

Holy Spirit in ministry. For only *through* the Holy Spirit can we discover what the Father is doing.

Jesus himself was able to know the Father's will and accomplish his ministry because he was radically dependent on the Holy Spirit. In the past, theologians generally neglected the role of the Holy Spirit in the ministry of Jesus. Focusing as they did on his relationship with the Father, they failed to give attention to the other relationship that defined his identity and mission—his relationship with the Holy Spirit. More recently, however, a number of theologians have been accentuating the vital role of the Holy Spirit in Jesus' life and ministry. Consider the following statement from a current ecumenical document on the Holy Spirit, which wonderfully draws together the many instances of the Holy Spirit's working in the life of Jesus: -

> Through love, the Holy Spirit orients the whole life of Jesus towards the Father in the fulfillment of his will. The Father sends his Son (Gal 4:4) when Mary conceives him through the operation of the Holy Spirit (Luke 1:35). The Holy Spirit makes Jesus manifest as Son of the Father by resting upon him at baptism (Luke 3:21-22; John 1:33). He drives Jesus into the wilderness (see Mark 1:12). Jesus returns "full of the Holy Spirit" (Luke 4:1). Then he begins his ministry "in the power of the Spirit" (Luke 4:14). He is filled with joy in the Spirit, blessing the Father for his gracious will (Luke 10:21). He chooses his apostles "through the Holy Spirit" (Acts 1:2). He casts out demons by the Spirit of God (Matt 12:28). He offers himself to the Father "through the eternal Spirit" (Heb 9:14). On the Cross he "commits his Spirit" into the Father's hands (Luke 23:46). "In the Spirit" he descended to the dead (1 Pet 3:19), and by the Spirit he was raised from the dead (Rom 8:11) and "designated Son of God in power" (Rom 1:4).[19]

There is no way, then, to account for Christ's ministry to the Father apart from his relationship to the Holy Spirit. As Peter declared, "God anointed Jesus of Nazareth with the Holy Spirit and with power" (Acts 10:38). Only through the Spirit was Jesus able to fulfill his mission.

The same was true for the leaders of the apostolic church. The risen Christ instructed them to wait for the outpouring of the promised Holy Spirit (Luke 24:49; Acts 1:4-8) before engaging in his work. On the Day of Pentecost they were all "filled with the Holy Spirit" (Acts 2:4) and began to minister in boldness and power. Throughout Acts, Luke describes various church leaders as being "filled with the Holy Spirit" (4:8; 6:3, 5; 7:55; 9:17; 11:24; 13:9), as though it were an essential requirement for ministry. And of course this raises the question: if it was an essential requirement for them, is it not also for us too?

What does it mean to be filled with the Holy Spirit? Although it is a spatial metaphor, being filled with the Spirit is not really about space, like filling up a cup with water. We will be misled if we conceive of it that way. Essentially this metaphor describes a personal relationship with the Holy Spirit characterized by surrender and abandonment to the Spirit. For though the Holy Spirit is present in all believers, in some he is not preeminent; though he is resident in all, in some he is not president. That is why Paul exhorts believers who already have a relationship with the Holy Spirit (Ephesians 1:13) to be filled with the Holy Spirit (Ephesians 5:18).

Richard Neuhaus says, "It is our determination to be independent by being in control that makes us unavailable to God."[20] Those who are filled with the Spirit have died to that determination, surrendered their right to be in control, and made themselves radically dependent on and available to the Holy Spirit. They have deliberately abandoned themselves to the Holy Spirit.

Only through such a relationship with the Holy Spirit are we enabled and empowered to participate in the ongoing ministry of Jesus and to discern what the Father wants us to do. Ministry, if it is to be fruitful—not merely productive—must be *through* the Holy Spirit. As E. Stanley Jones warns, "Unless the Holy Spirit fills, the human spirit fails."

Most of us give lip service to what Jones says but don't really believe it. We depend nominally on the Spirit but primarily on ourselves—our training, our skills, our personality, our past experiences, our knowledge, our sincere efforts. As a result, what we accomplish is limited to what we can do. As Wesley Duewel maintains, "If you rely on training, you accomplish what training can do. If you rely on skills and hard work, you obtain the results that skills and hard, faithful work can do. When you rely on committees, you get what committees can do. But when you rely on God, you get what God can do."[21]

Of course, ministry deserves our best—all that we have to offer. But it also demands more than our best, more than anything we have to offer. To participate in the ongoing ministry of Jesus, to do what the Father is doing, we must be filled with the Holy Spirit. Only through the Holy Spirit's directing and empowering us can we fulfill our calling.

According to Colin Gunton, on the day of his baptism Jesus "entered a new form of relationship with the Spirit."[22] Since he was conceived by the Holy Spirit (Luke 1:35), Jesus had a relationship with the Holy Spirit from the beginning of his earthly existence, but when the Spirit descended on him that day, his relationship with the Spirit expanded and deepened. Thus Jesus was able to overcome temptation in the wilderness (Luke 4:1-13) and preach good news to the poor (Luke 4:16-20). "Full of the Holy Spirit" (Luke 4:1), he was now ready to begin his ministry. The same holds true for us. Only when we have been filled with the Spirit and have entered into a deeper relationship with the Spirit are we ready to join Jesus in his ongoing ministry.

Billy Graham, whose life and work as an evangelist has been a wonderful example to so many in ministry, says it well: "I am convinced that to be filled with the Spirit is not an option but a necessity. It is indispensable for the abundant life and for fruitful service. . . . It is intended for all, needed by all, and available to all. That is why the Scripture commands all of us, 'Be filled with the Spirit.'"[23]

Of Jesus Christ, *to* the Father, *through* the Holy Spirit—this, then, is the ministry in the image of God to which we have been called. How inviting and demanding, how liberating and challenging it is! Ministry beckons us to enter into the triune life and to be conformed to it.

But we've only scratched the surface, only begun to grasp the richness of a trinitarian understanding of ministry. What else might it mean? In the chapters that follow, as we consider seven characteristics of trinitarian life and their implications for us, we will find out.

RELATIONAL PERSONHOOD

The Nature of Trinitarian Ministry

Because God is personal and not impersonal,
God exists as the mystery of persons in communion.

CATHERINE MOWRY LACUGNA

❖

After twenty-five years as a psychotherapist, professor, director of a counseling institute and author of bestselling books, Larry Crabb was a distinguished, respected leader in the field of Christian counseling. But in the mid-1990s, he shocked many of his colleagues when he openly questioned the value of much Christian psychotherapy and dared to suggest that the Christian counseling industry be dismantled. "You're committing professional suicide," a close friend warned him, yet Crabb continued speaking out.

In 1997 his groundbreaking book *Connecting* was published. In the introduction, Crabb boldly offered his prescription for healing soul wounds:

We must do something other than train professional experts to fix damaged psyches. Damaged psyches aren't the problem. The problem beneath our struggles is a disconnected soul. And we must do something more than exhort people to do what's right and then hold them accountable. Groups tend to emphasize accountability when they don't know how to relate. Better behavior through exhortation isn't the solution, though it sometimes is part of it. Rather than fixing psyches or scolding sinners, we must provide nourishment for the disconnected soul that only a community of connected people can offer.[1]

Our greatest need, he argued, is not for more Christian therapists and moralists but for authentic Christian communities, communities where "the heart of God is home, where the humble and wise learn to shepherd those on the path behind them, where trusting strugglers lock arms with others as together they journey on."[2]

Crabb urged America's churches to become such communities and to assume their indispensable role in healing wounded souls. Too often they have abdicated that role by simply referring people with emotional problems to therapists without providing them a vital community where healing can take place. Crabb also advised those working with broken people that therapy, discipleship and spiritual direction are more about relationships than about knowledge, programs or techniques. In 1977 he had written that "counseling is centrally and critically a relationship between people who care."[3] Now he was insisting that the relationship itself is what heals and nurtures human souls.

What prompted this change in Larry Crabb? Whether we completely agree with him or not, how do we account for his radical new vision? *Connecting* indicates that a number of factors—personal, spiritual, intellectual and theological—contributed to it. Above all, he had been brought to a profound awareness that human beings, created in the image of the triune God, are constituted for relationship. Crabb perceived that relational personhood, which characterizes the inner life of the Father, Son and Holy Spirit, is fundamental to human personhood as well.

This particular characteristic of trinitarian life is the focus of this chapter. Of all the seven characteristics we are considering, "relationality," as it's often called, has received the most attention in the recent trinitarian renaissance. Let's consider, then, how the Trinity reveals the relational nature of personhood. Then I'll draw out some of its implications for the vocation of ministry.

TRINITY AND PERSONHOOD

Ever since Augustine's *Confessions* with its introspective approach of searching for God within the human soul, we in the West have generally conceived of persons as separate selves with individual centers of consciousness. In the sixth century the Christian philosopher Boethius thus defined a person as "an individual substance of a rational nature."[4] His ancient definition has profoundly shaped our modern Western understanding where persons are viewed as free subjects who act on their own volition to establish relationships with others. Relationships, however, are not considered essential to personhood. They may be necessary for growth and maturity, but persons, as typically conceived, can exist *apart from* relationships.

That's why we generally define human dignity in terms of self-sufficiency and self-determination. Identity is conceived in self-referential terms, so that the authentic self is the inner self. Persons are autonomous and distinct from one another, determining their own goals and desires.

Such an understanding has led to the individualism and hyper-individualism that pervade American culture. As Robert Bellah observes, "Individualism lies at the very core of American culture. American individualism with its primary emphasis on self-reliance has led to the notion of pure, undetermined choice, free of tradition, obligation, or commitment, as the essence of the self."[5]

If, however, we begin with the triune God, existing as one in the communion of three persons, Father, Son and Holy Spirit, we arrive at a distinctively different understanding of personhood. The very names of the three persons imply existence in relationship. The Father is identified as Father only by virtue of his relationship to the Son, and vice versa. The Spirit is Spirit by virtue of his interaction with the other two. To think of the trinitarian persons, then, is to think of relations. The Father, Son and Holy Spirit are distinct persons by virtue of their relationships with one another. As Colin Gunton states, "God is no more than what Father, Son and Spirit give to and receive from each other in the inseparable communion that is the outcome of their love. . . . There is no 'being' of God other than this dynamic of persons in relation."[6]

Gunton goes on to distinguish a person, who is defined in terms of relations with other persons, from an individual, who is defined in terms of separation from other individuals. He also stresses that one person of the Trinity is "not the tool or extension of another." Though never separate from one another, the trinitarian persons are nevertheless distinct from one another. They never blend or merge or are subsumed by one another. Finally, there is freedom in their relations with each other—not freedom from the other persons (the typical Western conception) but freedom *for* the others, in which, paradoxically, the uniqueness and distinctiveness of each person finds its highest expression.[7]

Convinced that this trinitarian understanding of personhood is foundational to our understanding of human personhood, a growing number of theologians today, following the lead of early-twentieth-century theologians like Karl Barth, Emil Brunner and Dietrich Bonhoeffer, maintain that trinitarian personhood is the key to understanding the image of God (imago Dei) in humanity.[8] After all, the key biblical text for this doctrine says, "Let us make humankind in our image, according to our likeness" (Genesis 1:26). As Gunton maintains, "To be a person is to be made in the image of God: that is the heart of the matter. If God is a communion of persons inseparably related, then . . . it is in our relatedness to others that our being human consists."[9]

The being of a person is therefore being-in-relationship. Moreover, relatedness to others is two-dimensional: vertical (relatedness to God) and horizontal (relatedness to other humans and the rest of creation). Michael Downey summarizes what trinitarian theologians today are saying about human personhood:

> The human person is not an individual, not a self-contained being who at some stage in life chooses or elects to be in relationship with another and others. From the very first moment of existence, the infant is toward the other, ordinarily the mother or father, who is in turn toward and for the infant. From our origin we are related to others. We are from others, by others, toward others, for others, just as it is in God to exist in the relations of interpersonal love.[10]

But the Trinity not only reveals that persons are *essentially* relational, it also discloses characteristics that define healthy interpersonal relationships. In examining the portrait of the Trinity in the Gospel of John, Mark Shaw delineates four characteristics that define the relationships between the Father, Son and Holy Spirit: (1) full equality, (2) glad submission, (3) joyful intimacy and (4) mutual deference.[11]

For example, in John's prologue the Father and Son are presented as *equals* in that "the Word was with God, and the Word was God" (John 1:1). Yet though the Son enjoys a relationship of full equality with the Father, in *glad submission* he "became flesh and lived among us" (John 1:14). The Son *defers* to the Father by seeking to make the Father—not himself—known (John 1:18). He also enjoys *intimacy* with the Father, for he is "the only Son, who is close to the Father's heart" (John 1:18).

John 3 likewise reveals the glad submission and deference of the Son in relationship to the Father. "He whom God has sent speaks the words of God, for he gives the Spirit without measure" (John 3:34). The Son, then, doesn't venture to speak on his own but in glad submission speaks for the Father. Yet submission and deference is also reciprocal. The next verse states, "The Father loves the Son and has placed all things in his hands" (John 3:35).

In John 5 all four characteristics—equality, submission, deference and intimacy—appear again. The Jews wanted to kill Jesus because "he was not only breaking the sabbath but was also calling God his own Father, thereby *making himself equal to God*" (John 5:18). Deference of the Father to the Son is clearly stated in verses 22-23: "The Father judges no one but has given all judgment to the Son, so that all may honor the Son just as they honor the Father." Glad submission is apparent in verse 19: "Very truly, I tell you, the Son can do nothing on his own, but only what he sees the Father doing; for whatever the Father does, the Son does likewise." The joyful intimacy and oneness between the Father and the Son is revealed in verse 20, which asserts that "the Father loves the Son and shows him all that he himself is doing."

These four characteristics are also evident in John 8. Equality: "If you knew me, you would know my Father also" (v. 19), and "before

Abraham was, I am" (v. 58). Deference of the Son to the Father: "I do not have a demon; but I honor my Father" (v. 49). Deference of the Father to the Son: "If I glorify myself, my glory is nothing. It is my Father who glorifies me" (v. 54). Intimacy: "I do know him [the Father] and I keep his word" (v. 55). Glad submission: "And the one who sent me is with me; he has not left me alone, for I always do what is pleasing to him" (v. 29).

These characteristics are found again in John 10. Intimacy is revealed in verse 17, "For this reason the Father loves me, because I lay down my life in order to take it up again," and even more explicitly in verses 30, "The Father and I are one," and 38, "The Father is in me and I am in the Father." Jesus submits to the Father by showing his challengers "many good works *from the Father*" (v. 32, italics mine). As the Son speaks of his impending death, mutual deference is reflected in the Father's empowering of the Son and the Son's use of power only under the Father's authority: "No one takes [my life] from me, but I lay it down of my own accord. I have power to lay it down, and I have power to take it up again. I have received this command from my Father" (v. 18).

In the Upper Room Discourse, the intimacy, equality, deference and submission between the Father and the Son are shared with a third person—the Holy Spirit: "I will do whatever you ask in my name, so that the Father may be glorified in the Son. . . . And I will ask the Father, and he will give you another Advocate, to be with you forever" (John 14:13, 16). This relationship with the Spirit is also marked by equality. For the Spirit is "another Advocate"—not another *different* kind of Advocate, but another of the *same* kind, so that whatever Advocate Christ is, the Spirit is of the same essence. John 16 reveals the glad submission of the Spirit to the Son and the Father: "He will not speak on his own, but will speak whatever he hears. . . .

He will glorify me, because he will take what is mine and declare it to you. All that the Father has is mine. For this reason I said that he will take what is mine and declare it to you" (vv. 13-15).

Finally, in John 17, Jesus prays that those who believe in him may participate in the loving, deferring, enjoying and serving that characterize the fellowship of the Father, Son and Holy Spirit: "As you, Father, are in me and I am in you, may they also be in us. . . . The glory that you have given me I have given them, so that they may be one, as we are one . . . so that the love with which you have loved me may be in them, and I in them" (vv. 21-22, 26).

These four characteristics, then, define the relationships between the persons of the Trinity. As we shall see, they have significant implications both for healthy relationships in the church and for healthy family relationships. Of course, we must always remember that the triune relations are utterly unique *divine* relations. They are the original relations and the origin of all right relationships. We don't start with our human understanding of idealized relationships and project that onto God. Our starting point is the divine revelation of the triune relations, and that becomes a revelation to us of God's intention for human beings created in his image. However, because we humans are both finite and fallen creatures, our relationships, even when they are "in the Spirit," sharing in the triune life, will never be more than a dim reflection, a copy at best, of the original relationships in the Trinity. Still, the triune relations are the essential paradigm, our basic model for human relationships and relationships in the church.

RELATIONSHIPS IN THE CHURCH

In the light of trinitarian personhood and the four characteristics of triune relations, we could easily spend the rest of this chapter discussing relationships in the church. According to the New Testament, this is the primary arena where we are called to live out the triune model of relationality. In our fellowship, our *koinonia* (1 John 1:3), we not only share ourselves with one another but also share together in the triune life. Our diversity in unity mirrors the diversity in unity of the Trinity. Equality, intimacy, submission and deference ought to characterize relationships in the Christian community as well.

In the face of rampant American individualism, much could be said about developing ecclesial structures, practices and forms of leadership that nurture and enhance community. For the more these elements of church life are patterned after the Trinity, the more vital and fruitful our churches will become.

As a result of a comprehensive study (one thousand churches in thirty-two countries, on five continents), Christian Schwarz discovered that two of the eight essential characteristics of healthy, growing churches (holistic small groups and loving relationships) have to do directly with relationships.[12] Churches where persons are treated as objects, where ministry is executed in impersonal ways, stagnate and decline. In the light of the doctrine of the Trinity, that should come as no surprise to us. When the church's "life together" is patterned after and participates in the divine "life together," how can it not be life giving and life enhancing?

But make no mistake. Moving churches in the West toward a trinitarian model of church life will involve a major paradigm shift away from our pervasive individualistic ways of thinking. Many Christians have bought into the cultural notion that religion is an individual, private matter and assume they can believe without belonging. We have to say to them, "When you believed in Christ, whether you were aware of it or not, you entered into the fellowship of Father, Son and Holy Spirit, *and* the fellowship of every other Christian who is a part of that triune fellowship. Now you belong to everyone else who belongs. Your faith may be individual, but it's not personal except in relationship. In fact, you are only truly you in relationship to others." When we insist they are connected and call them to concrete relationships and practices that reflect their connectedness, we should expect resistance. Though people long for community, many are unwilling to count the cost necessary for it.

Much needs to be done, then, to flesh out relational personhood in the church. In *Community 101,* Gilbert Bilezikian attempts that. Beginning with the Trinity as "the original community of oneness," he envisions the local church as a community of oneness and draws out implications for small groups, church ministry and leadership.[13]

Unlike Bilezikian, this book has as its primary concern not the local church as a whole but those called to the vocation of ministry in the church. In considering the implications of relational personhood, I want to focus on three commitments it requires of us. First, a commitment to wholeness in our interpersonal relationships. Second, a commitment to involvement in close-knit small group fellowship. And third, a commitment to healthy family relationships.

OUR NEED FOR RELATIONAL WHOLENESS

As a result of their sin, all of Adam and Eve's relationships—with God, each other, themselves and the natural world—were radically affected. Living in the fallen world we inherited from them means living in a world of broken relationships. No matter, then, how much our parents and caregivers did right, especially during our years of infancy and childhood when our personhood was being shaped and established, all of us exhibit brokenness and unhealthiness in interpersonal relationships to one degree or another. These areas of relational dysfunction can have profound effects on our ministry. In fact, our most consequential failures in ministry are often failures in relationships. Who we are in our relationships with people generally trumps what we do for people.

Given what the Trinity tells us about the priority of relationships, this should come as no surprise. Most important, it should set us on a path from brokenness toward wholeness in our relationships with others.

How do relational problems manifest themselves? In his article "Trinity, Attachment and Love,"[14] Christian psychologist Stephen Stratton provides insightful answers by correlating contemporary trinitarian theology's understanding of personhood with attachment theory, the burgeoning psychological and neurobiological study of human relating. Similar to the trinitarian concept of being-in-relationship, attachment theory considers the dynamic balance of selves-in-relationship, without overemphasizing self or relations. Like the persons of the Trinity, human selves in proper relationships, rooted in love and characterized by dynamic interdependence, are never separate from one another nor subsumed by one another.

However, because we typically operate out of fear and self-protection rather than love, attachment theory sees us falling into two unhealthy relational styles. The first "finds its security in an overemphasis on relationships." Those who follow this strategy "often cling to sources of security and demand responsiveness, especially in times of distress." The second "finds its security in separation from others." Those who adhere to this strategy are "often counter-relational and may over-invest in what must be done around them rather than persons, particularly in difficult times."[15] Instead of living in a place of secure attachment, our self-protective efforts rooted in fear drive us either toward preoccupation with attachment (defensive dependence) or avoidance of attachment (defensive independence). In Miroslav Volf's words, we tend either toward unhealthy "embrace" or toward unhealthy "exclusion."[16]

Of course, mature interpersonal relationships include both. At times mature persons move toward exclusion, at other times toward embrace, depending on the person and the situation. Maturity comes as we cast out fear and learn to live out relationships dominated by love.

Which is your unhealthy tendency in interpersonal relationships? Mine has been toward an unhealthy exclusion that sometimes has caused me to substitute work for relationships. When I was forty years old, I began to deal with the childhood pain and fear underlying this.

I was born and raised in India, where my parents served as Methodist missionaries. In my office at the seminary where I teach hangs a painting of the lake at Kodaikanal, the scenic hill station in south India where I attended missionary boarding school during most of my elementary and junior high years. Kodaikanal was an ideal setting for such a school, and the years I spent there were positive in many ways. I received an excellent education and made lifelong friends. Committed Christian teachers and house parents provided me with positive role models.

But my years in boarding school were also emotionally painful. My parents lived five hundred miles away. When I was at school, our only communication was through letters. Being separated from them eight to nine months each year during that formative period of my life, I experienced profound loneliness. To halt the emotional pain, I made an inner vow: *I'll never need anybody ever again.* If you don't need anyone, I reasoned, then when they're not there it doesn't hurt as much.

As a teenager, Simon and Garfunkel's "I Am a Rock" was one of my favorite songs. Twenty-five years later I began to understand why. The lyrics that spoke of building walls and never needing friendship, of being a rock that feels no pain and an island that never cries, perfectly expressed what I had done.

When I was forty, God used a turbulent time in the life of one of my children to put me in touch with my childhood loneliness and the vow I had made in response to it. I saw with devastating clarity how it was affecting all my relationships. At a significant level I was emotionally unavailable to my wife and four children. I avoided deep friendships. Although it was easy for me to minister to others, it was difficult for me to acknowledge my own needs and receive ministry from others. My defensive independence also fueled an unhealthy absorption in work.

I will never forget the time in my office when several persons prayed with me about the protective fortress I had constructed around myself. I renounced the vow I had made never to need anyone and invited Jesus to come and minister to the lonely child within me.

Something within me shifted that day. The wall cracked and began to come down. As a result of that breakthrough, I embarked on a new path in my journey toward relational wholeness. Of course, I didn't change overnight. My relational patterns were deeply ingrained, so the process of dismantling the wall has been slow. But I have changed and am changing. I am learning to need people and give my heart to them in ways I never could before. I am moving from unhealthy, protective exclusion rooted in fear to healthy, open embrace rooted in love.

Your unhealthy relational tendency may be the opposite of mine, so you may need to move the other way—from fearful, enmeshed embrace toward loving exclusion and healthy boundary setting. A youth minister who was struggling with depression told me about a boy in his youth group who had recently tried to commit suicide. As we talked, it became clear that he was depressed because he had assumed responsibility for the boy's actions in an unhealthy way, as if somehow he was directly responsible for the boy's well-being. Consequently, when the boy tried to take his own life, the youth minister blamed himself. When I probed further, it was also evident that this was a relational pattern he had adopted since childhood—always taking upon himself responsibility for other people's happiness. There was a look of amazement on his face when he realized what he had been doing. Immediately he began to make the connection between his "codependent" relational tendency and his proneness to depression, people pleasing and workaholism. We prayed together that God would begin a process of transformation in him so that he could set healthy boundaries in his relationships with others.

Regardless of which relational direction you need to move (from protective exclusion or from enmeshed embrace), understanding trinitarian personhood should commit us to a journey toward wholeness in relationships with others.

SMALL GROUP INVOLVEMENT

But trinitarian personhood also means that we will never be able to complete that journey on our own. Since to be a person is to be in relationship with others, involvement in a small group of fellow Christians who are committed to us and to our journey together is indispensable to our spiritual and emotional growth.

When John Wesley was a young Christian, a "serious man" advised him, "Sir, you wish to serve God and go to heaven? Remember you cannot serve him alone. You must therefore find companions or make them. The Bible knows nothing of solitary religion."[17] In the light of the relational nature of personhood, that is good advice for every Christian, especially those involved in full-time ministry.

Wesley took that advice to heart both for himself and in shepherding the fledgling Methodist movement. Convinced that the pursuit of personal holiness was impossible apart from Christian community, he carefully organized the Methodists into societies (similar to congregations), classes (small groups of eight to twelve) and bands (cell groups of three to five).

Of these three structures, the bands are most directly relevant for our consideration here. Bands were voluntary cell groups of three to five deeply committed Christians who were passionate about growth in holiness and related deeply and regularly to each other. Unlike the societies and classes, bands were homogeneous in their makeup. By restricting them to persons of the same sex, age range and marital status, Wesley sought to create a context where persons felt free to be honest with one another and could share private things that would be inappropriate in larger, more diverse settings.

In his "Rules for the Bands," he clearly stated their purpose: "The design of our meetings is to obey that command of God, 'Confess your faults one to another, and pray for one another that ye may be healed' (James 5:16)."[18] Bands, therefore, functioned for both accountability and support. Members could speak openly about their failures and struggles in the pursuit of holiness without fear of rejection.

Because of the relational nature of human personhood, I believe every person in ministry needs to be in a small Wesleyan-type band group or its equivalent. Solitary religion is unbiblical; so is solitary service for God. We must either find companions or make them.

Yet many in ministry have no such group to which they belong. Of course they participate in congregational worship and may lead various kinds of small groups. But they are not involved in the kind of close, intimate band-type group I've been describing. Consequently, they have no place to go when they are weak, vulnerable or discouraged. They have no brothers or sisters in Christ with whom they can honestly bare their own soul, share their struggles, be challenged and held accountable, be supported and prayed for.

During eleven years in the pastorate, I was a part of several such groups and quickly realized how essential they were to my spiritual life and ministry. But for my first year and a half as a seminary professor, there was no such group functioning like this in my life. Although I knew it was lacking and I needed to find some spiritual companions among my faculty colleagues, I was hesitant to approach any of them for fear of rejection.

Then I heard Lloyd Ogilvie preach at our seminary's annual ministry conference. In his message he talked about a small group of several pastors he met with regularly. Over the years they had laughed and cried together, admonished one another and prayed together. At one point, when Ogilvie was extremely discouraged and wanted to quit, they said to him, "We won't let you give up. We're standing with you. If you go down, we're going down with you." Ogilvie encouraged us to become part of a group like that.

Prompted by what he said, I finally went to several faculty colleagues and asked them if they would be interested in forming such a group for sharing, encouragement, accountability and prayer. We've been meeting together ever since. When I think of all that we've been through together during the past two decades and all that my brothers Bob, Darrell and Reg have meant in my life, I am filled with awe and gratitude.

In his *Testament of Devotion* Thomas Kelly wonderfully captures what we have experienced as we've met together:

> Two people, three people . . . may be in living touch with one another through Him who underlies their separate lives. This is an astounding experience, which I can only describe but cannot explain in the language of science. But in vivid experience of divine Fellowship it is there. We know that these souls are with

us, lifting their lives and ours continuously to God and opening themselves, with us, in steady and humble obedience to Him. It is as if the boundaries of our self were enlarged, as if we were within them and as if they were within us. Their strength, given to them by God, becomes our strength, and our joy, given to us by God, becomes their joy. In confidence and love we live together in Him.[19]

As we've met together, Jesus has been true to his promise that when two or three of us gather in his name, he will be in our midst (Matthew 18:20), and through him, the Father and the Spirit as well! In our fellowship with one another, we have experienced a deep divine fellowship, the fellowship of the Trinity.

Are you part of a group like this? It may take time for you to "find [such spiritual] companions or [to] make them," but I encourage you to be patient and persistent until you do. You may need to move outside of your local church to find a group where you can be fully vulnerable. During my eleven years as a pastor I often found it necessary to do that, since some issues I was wrestling with in the church would have been unwise to talk about in the presence of other church members. Finding the time for a group for yourself can also be difficult. It may be helpful to schedule a breakfast or lunch meeting of your group.

HEALTHY FAMILY RELATIONSHIPS

A trinitarian understanding of personhood should also lead us to make family relationships a priority in ministry. As infants and children, we initially experienced the relational nature of personhood in our family. Now as adults, more than anywhere else, in our relationships with spouses and children we are made aware of our relational dysfunctions and provided with opportunities for growth.

What characterizes a healthy family? The four characteristics of trinitarian relationships discussed earlier—full equality, glad submission, mutual deference and joyful intimacy—all have significant implications for human family relationships. In fact, each is reflected in traits found in healthy families. Let's consider these four characteristics in the light of what family experts are saying.

Full equality. Like the persons of the Trinity, persons in healthy families can be distinguished from one another. The Father is not the Son, and the Son is not the Holy Spirit. A father is not a mother, and a mother is not a child. Yet all are persons. Equality, then, does not mean equivalence but a healthy respect for and valuing of the various members of the family and recognition of their full personhood.

Equality also implies respect for the boundaries of the various persons in the family. Salvador Minuchin has done extensive study of the role of boundaries in family systems.[20] Boundaries, he says, are invisible lines drawn within and among family members that define and structure interaction between husbands and wives, between parents and children, and between siblings. Boundaries also delineate the tasks, responsibilities and roles assigned to various family members. A clear boundary system is essential in developing healthy relationships in the family.

When family members don't respect each other's personal boundaries, they become overly enmeshed with one another. Enmeshment leads family members to inappropriately intrude on each other's thoughts, feelings and communications. As a result, development of full personhood is severely hampered.

An extreme example of enmeshed boundaries occurs in what Minuchin terms "anorectic" families, where members "seem like one body with three heads."[21] "They are enmeshed to the point that boundaries between people are far too weak to define and protect."[22] In such cases, children acknowledge no negative feelings toward their parents, allow parents to speak for them and are unable to perceive the severe dysfunction in their family. Proper boundaries are thus essential to family health, protecting and enhancing the equality of persons within the family.

Glad submission. According to Donald Joy, author of several books on the Christian family, in healthy families each member "looks out for each individual person's comfort, preferences, rights, and privileges, and goes in defense of protecting the person."[23] To do this they are willing to set aside their own wishes and engage in self-sacrifice, sometimes to great lengths, for the sake of another family member.

Healthy families are thus marked by a sacrificial, caring spirit toward others in the home, a spirit that often extends to those outside the family. By contrast, in unhealthy families the individual members are known for "placing self-interest ahead of any consideration of the rights or privileges of other people in the family."[24]

Mutual deference. Another characteristic of healthy families, according to Joy, is a high distribution of responsibility in the home. In family decision making, for example, high distribution of responsibility means including and seeking input from everyone and distributing power among everyone as well. Although roles may vary and power is not always distributed equally (parents will generally have more power than children; the husband may have more power than the wife, or vice versa, depending on the particular decision being made), still there is a desire that everyone participates in decision making, and power is shared. There is also willingness to defer to one another based on wisdom, experience and the nature of the situation at hand. By contrast, low distribution of responsibility indicates that one person is in control and makes the decisions for all the other family members.

Healthy families are also characterized by their ability to be flexible. Although they possess definite structures that provide consistency and stability, these structures are fluid so they can be changed or adapted. Husbands and wives, parents and children, may regularly assume roles that are reflected in certain patterns of behavior. Yet if the need arises, a role can be set aside as the primary responsibility of a particular person and assumed by someone else. In healthy families, the members don't cling to established roles out of fear of losing their identity or their power over others. They will defer to one another, so that everyone is empowered and the welfare of the family as a whole is enhanced.

Joyful intimacy. In healthy families, members highly value and enjoy one another. They desire to communicate with each other through words, touch, shared experiences, acts of kindness and time spent together. Being valued and enjoyed by others is exhilarating and enhances the self-worth of family members. Children nurtured in such an environment grow up being able to properly love and delight in themselves.

By contrast, members of unhealthy families often feel threatened by one another. Their relationships are marked by competition. Adults in such families suffer from low self-esteem, so they treat their spouse and children in demeaning ways to feel better about themselves. They use shame and humiliation as weapons to gain the upper hand over their children. Children follow their example in the way they relate to their siblings. They often grow up with a deep sense of shame and even despair about themselves and have difficulty functioning as adults.

Thus what characterizes the divine family—equality, submission, deference, intimacy—is reflected in healthy human families. As we consider our relationships with our spouse and children, do they reflect these trinitarian characteristics?

For many in ministry, this is their area of greatest failure. They would rather immerse themselves in work than spend time with their family. They sacrifice their family on the altar of ministry.

Like nothing else, family relationships expose our weaknesses and inadequacies. The work of ministry offers a tempting place to escape. There we feel strong, in control and appreciated—the opposite of how we often feel when we're with family members. Yet our existence and growth as persons is bound up with our relationships with them. Fleeing from our spouse and children to the work of ministry simply will not do. We must commit ourselves to the hard work of "life together" within the family.

Early in my ministry I discovered the power of the appointment book for setting apart time for our family. If a church committee proposed meeting on a given night, or if someone called asking if they could see me at a certain time, I would say, "Let me check my appointment book." After doing so, if I simply said, "I'm sorry, we can't meet then; I already have an appointment," they accepted it without question. It was as if what was in my appointment book was sacrosanct, something they dared not question or intrude upon. Having learned about the power of the appointment book (for you it may be a Palm Pilot), I began to use it to my advantage by writing down regular appointments with my family in it. This simple practice helped me protect my time with the family and make it a priority.

Are there specific practices you engage in to help cultivate family time? Do you take regular family vacations? Are you strict about taking days off or practicing sabbath? How many committees are you involved in? When it comes to our families, good intentions are not enough. We must be intentional and engage in specific practices if we are to give ourselves to our loved ones.

Relational personhood, therefore, has profound implications for the vocation of ministry. It commits us to wholeness in interpersonal relationships, to involvement in close-knit group fellowship and to the development of healthy family relationships. There is no place for disconnected lone rangers in ministry. If God is a communion of inseparably related persons, for us to exist as persons in ministry we must be in communion—in relationship—too.

THREE

JOYFUL INTIMACY

The Foundation of Trinitarian Ministry

This is the most beautiful moment of any creature's life:
to know that one is loved, personally, by God,
to feel oneself lifted to the bosom of the Trinity and to
find oneself in the flood of love that flows between the Father and Son,
enfolded in their love, sharing their passionate love for the world.

RANIERO CANTALAMESSA

❖

As a result of a dramatic conversion at the age of twenty-seven, Jack Frost was set free from addiction to drugs, alcohol and pornography. But it would take years before he was delivered from his deep-rooted fear of failure and the aggressive striving fueled by it.

As he became active in the church following his conversion, Frost simply transferred his fearful striving to religious work: "It seemed to be perfectly natural to express my love for God by building my identity through hyperreligious activity. Many of the Christians around me seemed to think the same way."[1] When he became a pastor, it only got worse:

My childhood filter system for earning love and acceptance translated ministry into an aggressive zeal to win souls and build the fastest-growing church in our denominational district.

I wanted to look good to everybody. But underneath the veneer of success, I was an unhappy man with a miserable family. My commitment to "the ministry" was far greater than my commitment to my wife, my children or any other loving relationships. When I was at home, I was irritable and impossible to get along with. Everything I did was tainted with passive anger.

My countenance became stern and serious, and my preaching became legalistic and demanding. . . . I knew the theology of God's love, but I had not experienced it in my relationships.[2]

Eventually Frost reached out for help. In 1986, during several intense healing prayer sessions, he faced the childhood roots of his anger, drivenness and lack of intimacy. Out of his newfound freedom and joy, he and his wife, Trisha, were soon conducting seminars in churches on emotional healing. However, Frost's struggle with performance orientation was still unresolved: "Even after we began the healing prayer ministry, I would often fall back into my old habit patterns of aggressive striving. I kept giving my wife those demeaning looks and speaking to her in stern and rigid tones. And when I was caught in this cycle, I couldn't see that I was the one at fault."[3]

Unable to measure up to his perfectionistic expectations, Frost's children didn't fare any better: "I would tell them I loved them, but I constantly pointed out every mistake and shortcoming. I demanded exact obedience, but I lacked the ability to express love, tender affection and grace and mercy when they fell short. . . . By 1995, my seventeen-year-old son and my fourteen-year-old daughter had closed their spirits to any affection, correction or advice I tried to offer them."[4]

Frustrated by his failures at home, Frost immersed himself in the one thing he did well—ministry. It was "all I talked about, all I lived for and all that brought a smile to my face."[5] But that only made matters worse.

With his family "teetering on the edge of disaster," Frost and his wife attended a conference on emotional healing in November 1995. During an afternoon session especially for pastors, Frost was kneeling with Trisha as she received prayer at the front. Someone on the platform began to pray, asking God to minister particularly to the men in the room whose human fathers hadn't been able to give them the love they needed. He recounts what happened next:

> It was as if God transported me back to a time when I was only ten. I suddenly saw vivid scenes of me as a child, hiding in a closet at night, fearful of the yelling and screaming I heard in my parents' room. I remembered the fear, the loneliness and the sense of abandonment. I felt the deep, painful ache for my father's embrace—an embrace he was not able to give me during my childhood.
>
> Suddenly I realized that now, thirty-four years later, my heavenly Father was meeting the deepest need in my heart for a natural demonstration of a father's affectionate love. I had a direct encounter with the *phileo* [affectionate love] of God. As I lay on the floor weeping, Father God entered that dark closet of my childhood and held me in His arms. For forty-five minutes, the Holy Spirit poured the love of God that the apostle Paul spoke of in Romans 5:5 through my body and washed away much of the guilt, shame, fear of failure and rejection, fear of intimacy and the fear of receiving and giving love.[6]

Frost's heartfelt experience of the Father's embrace transformed his family relationships. His wife gained a new husband—one who could finally open his heart to her in receiving and expressing love and pursuing deeper levels of intimacy. His children gained a new father. Although winning back their trust took considerable time, they immediately noticed the change. Four months after his encounter at the conference, his daughter, Sarah, expressed it like this: "He was Captain Bligh off the *H.M.S. Bounty.* Now he is gentle as a lamb, not to mention just as loving."[7]

Frost's approach to ministry was also transformed. As he describes it, "Ministry is no longer something that I have to work or strive for. . . . Most of the time I am motivated by a deep gratitude for being loved and accepted unconditionally by my Father. . . . As I receive His natural demonstration of affection for me, His precious *phileo* love, then I simply give it away to the next person I meet."[8]

Of course, Frost stresses that he has not "arrived" and has to be intentional about staying centered in the Father's love. When his priorities get confused, he soon finds himself falling into the old performance-oriented patterns. He has learned, however, to quickly run back to the resting place of God's love.

As a result of Frost's life-changing experience of the Father's embrace, Jack and Trisha Frost are now engaged in a full-time ministry to pastors and Christian leaders. Frost believes that, like himself, many persons in ministry need healing for deep emotional pain, but nothing heals a heart quicker than a profound encounter with divine love.

Sandra Wilson's story is not as dramatic as Frost's, but she too had a deep experience of intimacy with God that transformed her life and ministry. Both the adult child of an alcoholic and a sexual abuse survivor, she had become a gifted family therapist, adjunct seminary professor, author of numerous books, internationally sought speaker and respected leader in the field of Christian counseling. In the late

1990s she began writing a book on abandonment issues, but in the process, as she personally experienced new depths of intimacy with God, the focus shifted. What finally emerged, *Into Abba's Arms,* was primarily about cultivating intimacy with Christ in the face of abandonment.

Wilson's experience revolved around a change in her understanding and practice of certain Christian disciplines, especially prayer, silence and solitude. Before, prayer was mostly about her talking and God listening; now it was about her listening and God talking. As she notes, "I knew nothing of how to make 'listening prayer' an intentional part of my time with God. . . . So I began purposefully placing myself before the Savior to let him do some of the speaking in our prayer conversation. After all, a conversation is supposed to have *two* sides. I decided to record parts of these 'holy conversations' in my spiritual journal."[9]

It wasn't long before Wilson began to hear Christ speak words of intimate love such as these to her:

> *You are just beginning to get an inkling*
> *of what I mean when I say*
> *I love you.*
> *I mean I really love you!*
> *You matter to me.*
> *Those times when you are most enthralled—*
> *most moved with love for me—*
> *are but a dim reflection of*
> *how much I love you. . . .*
> *And no matter how wonderful,*
> > *how loving and merciful, you come to know I am,*
> > *I am far more.*[10]

As she continued to practice listening prayer, not only did her relationship with Christ take a quantum leap, but "somewhere deep inside, the ancient ache of abandonment also began to subside. It was as if—for the first time—I met my Immanuel. Jesus, God with *me,* became real. So did his promises of eternally nonabandoning love. I never anticipated what a profound change that would make in my life."[11] As a result, leading retreats and conferences on cultivating intimacy with Christ has become an important part of Wilson's ministry.

INTIMACY AND DELIGHT

Jesus prayed "that the love with which you [the Father] have loved me [the Son] may be in them, and I in them" (John 17:26). Jack Frost's and Sandra Wilson's experiences are concrete, unequivocal answers to his prayer. In trinitarian terms, they were enfolded, caught up in the love of the Father, Son and Holy Spirit for each other. In the next chapter we will consider this love's self-sacrificing nature. Now I want to focus on the joyful intimacy of this trinitarian love and its implications for ministry.

Jesus said that the Father's love for him (the Son) existed "before the foundation of the world" (John 17:24). The trinitarian persons have always had intimate communion and delightful fellowship with one another. As Wolfhart Pannenberg puts it, "From all eternity the Father loves the Son, the Son loves the Father, and the Spirit loves the Father in the Son and the Son in the Father. Each of the trinitarian persons loves the other, the Father the Son, the Son the Father, the Spirit both in fellowship."[12] Jürgen Moltmann calls it "an eternal love affair,"[13] and Leanne Payne speaks of "the Great Dance" of love between the persons of the Trinity.[14] Jon Tal Murphree elaborates further:

Each person of the Trinity identifies with the others. Each One transposes Himself into the others without confusing His own personality with the others. Through love, diversity and unity are so inextricably interwoven that the Father, Son, and Spirit do not exist as persons alongside each other as much as they exist in and through each other. Each One constantly has perfect access to the others' complete thoughts and feelings. Each is utterly transparent to the others, with no secretiveness. . . . In the Trinity, intimacy is complete![15]

John, the beloved disciple, conveys this intimacy at both the beginning and end of the prologue to his Gospel. "In the beginning was the Word," he says, "and the Word was *with* God" (John 1:1). The Greek preposition *pros* (translated "with") suggests both nearness and movement toward God.[16] "Face to face with God" is a literal translation. From all eternity, says John, the Son (the Word) and the Father (God) have existed not merely like side-by-side acquaintances, casually chatting with one another, but like face-to-face lovers, intently gazing into each other's eyes, engaged in joyful communion and intimate dialogue with each other.

The last verse of John's prologue declares that "God the only Son, who is close to the Father's heart, . . . has made him [God] known" (John 1:18). The Greek phrase translated "who is close to the Father's heart" literally says, "who is in the bosom of the Father," again suggesting nearness and intimacy.

And affection—the other aspect of trinitarian love I want to underscore. The persons of the Trinity are both near and dear to each other. They delight in each other; theirs is a joyful intimacy. As Roderick Leupp expresses it, "Divine joy powers the divine dance."[17]

Later in his Gospel, when Jesus says, "The Father loves the Son and shows him all that he himself is doing" (John 5:20), John again emphasizes the affectionate dimension of trinitarian love. In describing the love of the Father for the Son, John generally uses the Greek verb *agapeo,* which accentuates the sacrificial nature of that love. In this case, however, he uses *phileo,* which, more than *agapeo,* connotes the brotherly love and tender affection of friends and family members. By using *phileo,* John underscores the joyful affection and delight of the Father for and in the Son.

Jesus' use of the Aramaic word *Abba* when he prayed to his heavenly Father in Gethsemane (Matthew 26:39; Mark 14:36) combines both aspects of trinitarian love (nearness and dearness, intimacy and delight). There is good reason to believe that he often addressed God this way.[18]

Abba was the familiar name Jewish children used in addressing their fathers. The best English translation for it is "Daddy" or "Dearest Father." No Jewish rabbi ever had the audacity to address Almighty God in such an informal, intimate way. *Abba* expressed trust, belonging and intimacy—a tender, affectionate love that enjoys and embraces the beloved. Calling God *Abba* was new and revolutionary.

However, Jesus was merely revealing what has always been: in the beginning, face to face with God, the Father, Son and Holy Spirit in joyful, intimate fellowship, eternally near and dear to one another.

What is new and revolutionary is that now we too, through faith in Christ, are enfolded in that divine fellowship and join in the dance! God has not left us outside the circle of his trinitarian life. We are invited, as it were, inside the circle of intimate, delightful trinitarian love. As John of the Cross poetically exclaims:

There to be rapt as God is
seized by the same delight

for even as father and son
and the third, not less in might,

one in the other endure
so with the fond and fair—
caught into God's great being,
breathing his very air![19]

Through the Holy Spirit, the third person of the Trinity, we are drawn into the circle of this love. The Spirit pours the love of God into our hearts (Romans 5:5), cries in us "Abba, Father," and bears witness with our spirits that we are God's children (Romans 8:15-16; Galatians 4:6). The Spirit, as Augustine emphasized, is the bond of love between the Father and the Son. His triune identity is closely linked to the communion of mutual and reciprocal love that flows between the Father and the Son. The Spirit is in the love they share and can even be thought of as the channel of their loving.

No wonder that when we enter the trinitarian circle, it is the Holy Spirit who both communicates God's love to us and enfolds us in its dynamic movement. Clark Pinnock captures it well: "Spirit is content to be thought of as the medium and fellowship of love. He delights in the loving relationships of the divine dance and exults in the self-emptying love that binds Father and Son. He delights to introduce creatures to union with God, the dance of the Trinity and the sabbath play of new creation."[20]

The Spirit also delights when we subjectively experience the divine embrace, when we actually sense the joyful intimacy of trinitarian love. Paul has this in mind when he says, "You have received a spirit of adoption. When we cry, 'Abba! Father!' it is that very Spirit bearing witness with our spirit that we are children of God" (Romans 8:15-16). The Greek verb *krazo*, translated "cry" or "cry out," implies an intensity of feeling, a deep emotive response. As New Testament scholar James Dunn explains, "The Spirit is here spoken of in irreducibly emotional and experiential terms."[21] The Spirit, then, desires to communicate to us a deep conscious awareness that we are God's children, his dearly loved sons and daughters.

Once when I was praying with a woman we'll call Janet, I witnessed the Spirit doing this. A week before, she had been visiting a friend who had recently had a baby. While we were praying, the Spirit brought to mind her sense of wonder, joy and delight as she snuggled the newborn in her arms. Then the Spirit whispered, "Do you remember how you felt last week when you held your friend's baby? That's how I, your Heavenly Father, feel toward you, Janet. You are a beloved daughter to me."

Jesus himself experienced an intense, intimate awareness of his sonship when he was baptized. As he was coming out of the water, the Holy Spirit descended on him and a voice from heaven declared, "You are my Son, the Beloved; with you I am well pleased" (Mark 1:11). Thus the Father confirmed Jesus as his Son and chosen servant (echoing messianic titles found in Psalm 2:8 and Isaiah 42:1). And he also named him "the Beloved," a special term of endearment that communicated tender, intimate love.

Jesus, then, was firmly convinced of the Father's intimate love and affection for him. He *knew* he was dearly loved. That's why, soon afterward when he was tempted, he refused Satan's challenge to prove he was the Son of God by turning stones into bread and jumping from the pinnacle of the temple. As Henri Nouwen suggests, "Jesus . . . is very clear in his response: 'I don't have to prove that I am worthy of love. I am the Beloved of God, the One on whom God's favor rests.'"[22]

The Foundation of Ministry

Jesus heard the Father's affirming voice and felt his embrace at the very beginning of his public ministry. In fact, his profound awareness of the Father's affectionate love was the foundation of his ministry. Through his ministry, he never sought to establish his worth. It was rooted in his confidence in his belovedness. Doing was the result of being (in a relationship with the Father), not the other way around. As Frank Lake observes, "For Christ his Spiritual 'Being,' as Son of God, arises in a relationship between the Father Who attends with love, mediated by the Holy Spirit, given to Him without measure, and the Son Who responds to the Father by the same Spirit."[23]

In his seminal work *Clinical Theology*, Lake, a psychiatrist and pastoral theologian, studies the person of Christ as reflected in the four Gospels in order to develop a model to delineate what he terms "the Dynamic Cycle of Being," arising out of healthy interpersonal relationships. He describes four dynamic elements of the Father-Son relationship that established and sustained Christ's personhood. The first two constitute an "input phase," the last two an "output phase."

1. *Acceptance.* The Son hears the voice from heaven, "You are my Son, the Beloved" (Mark 1:11). From the beginning, his acceptance by the Father and his sense of being as the Son are never in question. Jesus repeatedly refers to himself as the Son. He does nothing to earn the relationship. When he withdraws to pray, he has instant access to his Father.

2. *Sustenance.* The Son is loved by the Father (John 15:9). His Father is well pleased with him (Mark 1:11) and gives sustenance to his being on all levels as he conveys to the Son a plenitude of love, glory, joy, grace and truth. The Father's enjoyment of him bestows on the Son a sense of well-being.

3. *Status.* Out of his profound sense of being and well-being, the Son "proceeds from the presence of His Father, full of grace and truth, deeply conscious of His status as the Son of God, to work among men."[24] He is from above (John 8:23), sent by God to do God's work (John 7:18, 28), the living bread (John 6:51), the water of life (John 7:37), the light of the world (John 8:12). Everything has been entrusted to him by the Father (John 13:3).

4. *Achievement.* The Son has been given a task and through the indwelling Holy Spirit (Luke 4:18-19) is able to accomplish it. He is also able to engage in purposeful activity and experience joyful expression and achievement in work. He fulfills his redemptive destiny by finishing the work the Father has given him to do (John 17:4).

Lake's model clearly demonstrates that Christ's ministry is rooted in his grace-given identity. Jesus is declared to be the Father's beloved Son in whom he is well pleased *before* he begins to preach, teach and heal. His mighty works and laying his life down are not motivated by a need to earn acceptance or status from his Father or to fill up anything lacking in his sense of being. Instead they flow out of his fullness of being, rooted and sustained by his joyful, intimate love relationship with his Father.

Since our ministries are patterned after and participate in Christ's ministry, the four dynamic elements constitutive of Christ's personhood and ministry should be constitutive of ours too. Acceptance and sustenance, the input phase, are first and foundational. The Father's love is poured into our hearts through the Holy Spirit and communicates to us the Father's approval and delight. This leads to status and achievement, the output phase, which involves acknowledging our acceptance and accomplishing the work the Father has called us to do.

Too often persons enter ministry without this proper foundation firmly established. Consequently they make their achievement, their work for God, the foundation of their ministry, rather than their acceptance and approval by God. Wanting to *do* something in order to *be* someone, they view themselves, in Mike Bickle's words, as "loving workers" instead of as God intends, as "working lovers." Bickle, founding director of the International House of Prayer of Kansas City, maintains, "God wants us to be something *before* He wants us to do something. . . . God wants us to be lovers so that we do work."[25] So Jesus asks Peter "Do you love me?" before he commands him to "Feed my sheep" (John 21:15-17). The order is significant.

Tammy Hutchins came to a profound realization of this while she was on a mission trip to India in June 1997. I was a part of that mission trip too. It was the first time I had been back to India since leaving in 1962, so in addition to the ministry we were involved in, it was a wonderful time of reconnecting for me. Tammy, on the other hand, had never been to India, but having just graduated from seminary, she was sensing a call to minister to orphaned and abandoned children there. So this was an initial, exploratory trip for her. She wanted to experience the sights and sounds of India and confirm the direction God was leading her.

However, after several days in India, Tammy was overwhelmed. The grinding poverty, endless rows of squatter houses, street children and beggars, corruption, idolatry, hopelessness, and spiritual darkness were beyond anything she had imagined. "Lord," she prayed, "I don't really like this country. It's too hard. Yet I believe I've felt your call here. I'm confused. What am I going to do?"

Tammy realized that all the human love and compassion she could muster would soon be depleted in India. If God wanted her to serve there, she would need his love and compassion to sustain her. In a home where she was staying, a large map of India hung on the wall. Each time she would look at it, Tammy prayed, "Lord, please give me your heart for India."

One day as she was praying, the Lord spoke to her clearly. "How can I give you my heart for India," he asked, "when you don't even know my heart for you?"

At first Tammy was evasive: "God, you don't understand: I want your heart for India. I didn't come on this mission trip for myself. I just want your heart for India so I can serve you here."

But the Lord persisted: "Tammy, how can I give you my heart for India when you don't even know my heart for you?"

During the rest of her time in India, God gave Tammy a deeper revelation of his heart for her. And in giving her what she hadn't asked for—God's heart for her—she also received what she had asked for: God's heart for India. As she describes it,

> He began to pour out His love for me in fresh ways! Early on in my walk with Christ, I had known in my *mind* that Jesus loved me. Over the past three years at seminary, He has revealed the depths of His love for me in my *heart*. During my month in India, He poured out His love in a new measure. I experienced His love for me in the innermost part of my *being*. . . . I started out praying for God's heart for India. He revealed the realness of His heart for me, and because of this incredible truth, He is giving me the very thing I asked for, His heart for India.[26]

Six months later Tammy returned to India, and she has been ministering there ever since. God is using her in amazing ways to communicate his unfailing love to the despised and unwanted. During that initial trip, the foundation of her ministry was properly established. As she explains when she tells her story, "Before you can have God's heart for others, you must know His heart for you."

A firm grasp of the Father's joyful, intimate love for us is the foundation of ministry, but we also need continued experiences of his love. So Paul prays that those who are already "rooted and grounded in love" may comprehend "what is the breadth and length and height and depth, and to know the love of Christ that surpasses knowledge" (Ephesians 3:17-19). Without regular experiences of the Father's embrace, we forget whose we are and our focus shifts from relationship to work. Working for God becomes more important than loving God. What we *do* for God becomes more important than who we *are* as his beloved sons and daughters.

Craig Keener, professor of New Testament at Eastern Baptist Seminary, tells about a time when the pressures of trying to find time for teaching, writing and speaking were overwhelming him. During a worship service, God's Spirit spoke to his heart: "My son, you will not always have this ministry or that ministry. These gifts will pass away when you stand before me. But you will *always* be my son."[27] Keener wept as he felt the comfort of the Father's embrace. He also felt a gentle reproof as he realized that, like distracted Martha (Luke 10:40), he had gotten so wrapped up in his work for God he was neglecting his love relationship with God. Although he sensed that the Lord was pleased with his work, he recognized that more than his work, the Lord desired his fellowship. "I won't always be a teacher or a writer," says Keener, "but I will always be his child, and that means more to me than anything else."[28]

We all need such heartfelt experiences now and then to remind us that first and foremost we are God's beloved daughters and sons. We also need regular times of prayer and devotion where, like undistracted Mary (Luke 10:39), we sit at the feet of Jesus and commune intimately with him. As Brennan Manning maintains, "The indispensable condition for developing and maintaining the awareness of our belovedness is time alone with God. . . . There we discover that the truth of our belovedness is really true."[29]

At his baptism, Jesus heard his Father's voice: "You are my beloved Son." We need to regularly hear it, too. I've learned that if I fail to regularly spend time alone with God, soon I am hearing other voices, especially those of the world system around me and my own dysfunctional self-talk. Instead of hearing, "Steve, you are my beloved son," I'm hearing voices that declare, "You are how much you produce . . . you are how well liked you are . . . you are how large your ministry is . . . you are how well known you are." And soon, "You are my beloved son" ceases to define my identity and determine my direction, and those other "you ares" are doing it.

There is no substitute for time alone with God, when we attune ourselves to God's voice reminding us once again of how beloved we are.

REMOVING BARRIERS TO RECEIVING GOD'S LOVE

Since knowing the Father's joyful, intimate love is foundational for ministry, we need to ask God to reveal barriers that prevent us from experiencing his love and to help us remove them. Jack Frost's story at the beginning of this chapter illustrates how unhealed hurts of the past, especially from childhood, can erect barriers to joyful intimacy with God. The healing of Frost's heart, wounded by his demanding, distant earthly father, removed a critical barrier that had kept him from experiencing his heavenly Father's embrace.

Charles Stanley, the well-known television preacher and longtime pastor of First Baptist Church in Atlanta, experienced a similar healing that removed a barrier to intimacy with God. During a time of healing prayer when several close friends ministered to him, Stanley was set free from deep feelings of rejection rooted in the loss of his father when he was only seven months old. Here's how he describes what happened:

> One of these fellows said, "Charles, put your head on the table and close your eyes." So I did. Then he said to me very kindly, "Charles, your father just picked you up in his arms and held you. What do you feel?" I burst out crying. And I cried and I cried, and I could not stop crying. Finally, when I stopped, he asked me again, and I said that I felt warm and loved and secure and good, and I started weeping again. For the first time in my life I felt God emotionally loving me. All these years I had preached about trusting God and believing him and obeying him. And I had. But I came back and I looked through my sermon file, and in all of those years I had only preached one sermon on the love of God and it was not worth listening to. The reason was because I didn't know what it meant to feel the love of God because my daddy had walked out on me in death at seven months of age.[30]

Like Stanley, you may have childhood emotional wounds that make it difficult for you to experience joyful intimacy with God. In the previous chapter I described the wall I had constructed around my own heart to silence the deep ache of loneliness I felt during my years in missionary boarding school. Brick by brick, as that wall has been dismantled, my awareness of my belovedness and my heartfelt experiences of the Father's love have increased in frequency and intensity.

Do you need healing for childhood wounds? Let me encourage you to do all that's necessary on your part—honestly facing past wounds, forgiving those who hurt you, seeking out others who can listen and counsel and pray with you, bringing your hurts to the cross where Christ's wounds can touch yours—to receive healing so that you can experience the Father's embrace in greater measure.[31]

Along with wounds from childhood, wounds inflicted on us during the course of ministry, especially when we are being obedient to God, can create barriers to intimacy with God. Consider, for example, what happened to Moses at the beginning of his ministry. When God first spoke to Moses at the burning bush and told him he would be the deliverer who lead the people out of slavery in Egypt, Moses resisted and didn't hesitate to voice his objections: I'm not qualified (Exodus 3:11). I don't know what to say if they ask me your name (Exodus 3:13). The people won't believe me or listen to me (Exodus 4:1). I'm not eloquent (Exodus 4:10).

God, however, patiently reassured Moses and responded to his concerns one by one. He even granted Moses' request to allow his brother, Aaron, to accompany him and be his spokesman. So, finally, Moses reluctantly agreed to go.

Upon his arrival in Egypt, Moses first met with the Israelite leaders. When he told them what God had sent him to do, they were overjoyed. At long last God had answered their prayers. Moses, the long-awaited deliverer, had arrived. How thrilled they were that he had finally come.

But not for long! When he went to Pharaoh and commanded him to let the people go, Pharaoh adamantly refused. To make matters worse, he increased the Israelite workload, demanding that they produce bricks without straw. And when they failed to meet their quota, the Israelite foremen were beaten.

Then the people turned on Moses and raged against him. All this was his fault. Some deliverer he turned out to be. It would have been better if he had never showed up.

Wounded by their attack and confused by what had happened, Moses turned on God. His complaint is recorded for us in Exodus

5:22-23: "O LORD, why have you mistreated this people? Why did you ever send me? Since I first came to Pharaoh to speak in your name, he has mistreated this people, and you have done nothing at all to deliver your people."

Commenting on Moses' distraught reaction, Bible expositor J. Sidlow Baxter makes the application to us:

> Have we not all had experiences of a like kind? We have felt the unmistakable urge of the Spirit to some new form of service, or to some special line of action, and have obediently pressed forward, confident that the inward urge itself was the guarantee of immediate success. Then, instead of success, opposition and disappointment and seeming failure have stunned us into bewildered despair, until we have even been ready to fling the charge of unfaithfulness in the face of God.[32]

Like Moses, in the course of ministry we too will have experiences like this. And when we've been wounded on account of our obedience to God, when we feel abandoned by God, it is difficult to trust God, let alone receive his love. Situations like this fuel anger toward God and cause us to pull away from him.

A pastor told me how this happened to him. He had left a large church, which had grown significantly over his twelve-year ministry, to pastor the church he was currently serving. It was a smaller church than the one he had left, but because God had led him there in such a clear and unmistakable way, he was certain God would use him to grow this congregation just like the last one. Now, however, after eight years of ministry there, the congregation had declined by nearly 30 percent! He described his growing sense of disillusionment with God:

> Every year I would prop up my optimism, call the church to prayer, plan a new strategy, and then be disappointed with the

results. Remembering the call, I refused to give up. But slowly, without realizing it, I began to become very disappointed with God. I quit praying. After all, what was the point? God didn't seem to be listening anyway. I really felt like God had forsaken me. In time, my soul became empty and dry and I reached out to a mentor/friend who helped me to identify my deep disappointment with God.

Having encountered opposition, criticism, disappointment and failure, you may be in such a place. Your heart has been wounded and needs to heal. And generally such wounds hurt more deeply and heal more slowly than we like to admit. In the process, you will need to honestly acknowledge the depth of your hurt, forgive those who have inflicted the wounds, own your disappointment and even anger toward God, and invite Jesus to mend your heart. As this happens, you will gradually be able to trust again and open your heart to God and others.

In the meantime, as you tread the path toward healing, know that whether you are feeling his embrace or not, the Father's love for you, like his love for his only Son, is steadfast and relentless. Although you may not be hearing them, the Father sings love songs over you. According to the Scripture, "he will rejoice over you with gladness, he will renew you in his love" (Zephaniah 3:17).

As I've emphasized throughout this chapter, this joyful, intimate love for us is rooted and grounded in the love the persons of the Trinity have for one another. Andrew Murray captures it well: "The love of the Father to the Son is that divine passion which delights in the Son, and speaks, 'My beloved Son, in whom I am well pleased.' The divine love is as a burning fire; in all its intensity and infinity it has but one object and but one joy, and that is the only-begotten Son."[33]

Jesus came so that we can be included in the circle of that fiery love. The Father, he declares, loves us as the Father loves the Son (John 17:26), and the Son, in turn, loves us as the Father loves him (John 15:9). Murray spells out the staggering implications for us:

> This love of God to His Son must serve, O my soul, as the glass in which you are to learn how Jesus loves you. As one of His redeemed ones, you are His delight, and all His desire is to you, with the longing of a love which is stronger than death, and which many waters cannot quench. His heart yearns after you, seeking your fellowship and your love. . . . His life is bound up in yours; you are to Him inexpressibly more indispensable and precious than you can ever know.[34]

And this love—so amazing, so divine—is the only sure foundation of ministry, the overflowing fountain out of which our love for God and for others arises. Has that foundation been firmly established in your life and ministry? Do you need to plunge deeper into the fountain of trinitarian love? Are there wounds from the distant or recent past that need the healing balm of that love?

Pray then for a renewed experience of God's love. Ask that it might be shed abroad in your heart by the Holy Spirit once again. May the following verses from Charles Wesley's hymn express the desire of your heart:

> O love divine, how sweet thou art!
> When shall I find my willing heart
> All taken up by thee?
> I thirst, I faint, I die to prove
> The greatness of redeeming love,
> The love of Christ to me!

God only knows the love of God;
O that it now were shed abroad
In this poor stony heart!
For love I sigh, for love I pine:
This only portion, Lord, be mine,
Be mine this better part!

O that I could for ever sit
With Mary at the Master's feet,
Be this my happy choice:
My only care, delight, and bliss,
My joy, my heaven on earth be this,
To hear the bridegroom's voice!

O that I could, with favored John
Recline my weary head upon
The dear Redeemer's breast!
From care, and sin, and sorrow free,
Give me, O Lord, to find in thee
My everlasting rest.[35]

GLAD SURRENDER

The Heart of Trinitarian Ministry

So self-surrender is at the very heart of God
and is at the very heart of all his attitudes and actions.
When He asks us to surrender ourselves He is asking us
to fulfill the deepest thing in Himself and the deepest thing in us.

E. STANLEY JONES

❖

In Hannah Hurnard's popular spiritual allegory *Hinds' Feet on High Places*, Much-Afraid is puzzled when she learns that she is ascending to the High Places not to remain there forever but so she can descend back into the Valley of Humiliation from which she has fled. At the beginning of her journey with the Shepherd, as they cross a swift stream running through the valley, he bids her listen to the words being sung by the rushing water: "*Come, oh come! Let us away—Lower, lower every day. . . . From the heights we leap and flow, To the valleys down below, Sweetest urge and sweetest will, To go lower, lower still.*"

The water sings joyfully as it hurries down to the lowest place, yet the Shepherd is calling Much-Afraid to ascend to the High Places. It seems contradictory, so Much-Afraid asks what it means. "The High Places," the Shepherd explains, "are the starting places for the journey down to the lowest place in the world. When you have hinds' feet and can go 'leaping on the mountains and skipping on the hills,' you will be able, as I am, to run down from the heights in gladdest self-giving and then go up to the mountains again . . . for it is only on the High Places of Love that anyone can receive the power to pour themselves down in an utter abandonment of self-giving."[1] At this point in her journey, however, Much-Afraid is perplexed by the Shepherd's answer.

Later, though, when they arrive at the borderland of the High Places, she begins to understand. Standing before the towering cliffs still to be scaled, the Shepherd has Much-Afraid look up at the mighty waterfall flowing down from the High Places. When she does, she is awed by the tremendous height of the rocky lip over which the water cascades down and the deafening noise as it crashes down on the rocks at the foot of the fall. Never has she seen anything "so majestic or terrifyingly lovely."[2] Once again, as in the valley, she hears the waters singing, *From the heights we leap and go, To the valleys down below, Always answering to the call, To the lowest place of all.*

To Much-Afraid the fall of the mighty waters is both beautiful and terrible. She can hardly bear to watch the water cast itself down from the heights above only to be shattered on the rocks beneath. Sensing her apprehension, the Shepherd urges her to look more closely: "Let your eye follow just one part of the water from the moment when it leaps over the edge until it reaches the bottom."[3]

As she does, she gasps in wonder: "Once over the edge, the waters were like winged things, alive with joy, so utterly abandoned to the ecstasy of giving themselves that she could almost have supposed that she was looking at a host of angels floating down on rainbow wings, singing with rapture as they went."[4] To the water this was the loveliest, most glorious movement in the world. And its joy didn't end when it broke upon the rocks below. In fact, the lower the water fell, the lighter and more exuberant it became. A rushing torrent, it swirled triumphantly around the rocks and then flowed downward, lower and lower, around and over every obstacle in its way.

As the Shepherd explains:

At first sight perhaps the leap does look terrible . . . but as you can see, the water itself finds no terror in it, no moment of hesitation or shrinking, only joy unspeakable and full of glory, because it is the movement natural to it. Self-giving is its life. It has only one desire, to go down and down and give itself with no reserve or holding back of any kind. You can see that as it obeys that glorious urge the obstacles which look so terrifying are perfectly harmless, and indeed only add to the joy and glory of the movement.[5]

Soon Much-Afraid discovers firsthand what this means. After she ascends to the High Places and is given a new name (Grace and Glory), compassion for those in the Valley of Humiliation wells up within her. They are so fearful and bound; she longs to tell them how the Bridegroom-King can free them as he freed her.

As she rises to go down into the Valley, she sees the great waterfall and hears the song again: "*From the heights we leap and flow, To the valleys down below, Sweetest urge and sweetest will, To go lower, lower still.*" Now she fully understands. She has been brought by the King to the High Places so she too can pour herself out in joyful abandonment: "The thought of being made one with the great fall of many waters filled her heart with ecstasy and with a rapturous joy beyond power to express. She, too, at last was to go down with them, pouring herself forth in love's abandonment of self-giving. 'He brought me to the heights just for this,' she whispered to herself, and then looked at him and nodded."[6]

What Much-Afraid once considered terrible, "love's abandonment in self-giving," has become to her altogether lovely, a fountain of unspeakable joy. What she has shrunk away from for fear of losing herself, she now gladly embraces as the grand purpose of her existence.

Much-Afraid's discovery is the focus of this chapter. For what she comes to understand and experience is merely a dim reflection, a shadow, of the eternally unfolding reality of "love's abandonment in self-giving" among the persons of the Trinity. "Self-giving love," as Roderick Leupp emphasizes, "is the Trinity's signature."[7] This characteristic is at the heart of triune life.

SURRENDER AND SELF-GIVING IN THE TRINITY

To demonstrate the depth of God's sacrificial self-giving love for humanity, the New Testament writers always point to a concrete, historical event: Christ's death on the cross. "God proves his love for us," declares Paul, "in that while we still were sinners Christ died for us" (Romans 5:8). Similarly John writes, "In this is love, not that we loved God but that he loved us and sent his Son to be the atoning sacrifice for our sins" (1 John 4:10).

But Christ's death not only supremely reveals the nature of divine love, it also discloses what is eternally etched in the heart of the triune God. *Before* creation, before the existence of a world in need of redemption, self-giving, self-sacrificing love marked the fellowship of the Father, Son and Holy Spirit. Jesus, the Lamb of God who died on Calvary to take away sins, is the Lamb slain *from the foundation of the world* (Revelation 13:8).

The obedience and humiliation of the Son, culminating in his death on the cross, are thus a revelation of the inner life of God. "The cross," as Jürgen Moltmann suggests, "is at the center of the Trinity.

. . . Before the world was, the sacrifice was already in God. No Trinity is conceivable without the Lamb, without the sacrifice of love, without the crucified Son. For he is the slaughtered Lamb glorified in eternity."[8] Likewise, according to Rowan Williams, the amazing love displayed in the self-emptying of God on Good Friday is "no arbitrary expression of the nature of God: this is what the life of the Trinity is, translated into the world."[9]

In chapter one we considered the angelic figures in Rublev's icon, which so marvelously portrays the nature of the Trinity and invites us into the circle of trinitarian fellowship. However, when we step back from the icon to perceive its overall structure, something startling slowly emerges. "Gradually," Henri Nouwen observes, "a cross is becoming visible, formed by the vertical beam of the tree, the Son, the Lamb and the world, and by the horizontal beam, including the heads of the Father and the Spirit."[10]

Rublev's icon of the Trinity portrays two overarching forms, a circle of joyful, intimate relationships and a cross of self-sacrificing love, which are inextricably bound together. As Nouwen emphasizes, "There is indeed no circle without a cross, no life eternal without death, no gaining life without losing it, no heavenly kingdom without Calvary. Circle and cross can never be separated. The severe beauty of the three divine angels is not a beauty without suffering."[11]

In chapter two we observed that in the portrait of the Trinity found in John's Gospel, "glad submission" and "mutual deference" characterize the relationships between the Father, Son and Holy Spirit. Each divine person is always denying himself for the sake of the others and deferring to the others. The Father gives up his only Son for the sake of the world (John 3:16; Romans 8:32). The Son never seeks to do his own will but only the will of the Father (John 4:34; 5:19; 6:38). The Spirit, in turn, seeks only to glorify the Son and the Father (John 16:13-15).

John, of course, underscores the self-giving and deferring nature of the triune persons in relation to what God has done to redeem and restore the fallen world. In his Gospel he is primarily concerned with what theologians term the *economic* Trinity—the actions of the triune God in creation and redemption. However, self-giving and mutual deference define their actions not only in creating and redeeming the world but also among themselves from all eternity.

Before creation, in their eternal trinitarian life together (what theologians call the *immanent* Trinity), their relationships are characterized by glad submission and deference to one another. There is no egocentricity within the Godhead, nothing that is self-serving or self-seeking. Each of the triune persons freely lays himself down for the sake of the other two and, in the very act of losing his life, finds it in eternal joyous communion with the others. As theologian Geoffrey Wainwright explains, "The divine Persons empty themselves into each and receive each other's fullness."[12]

According to theologian Wolfhart Pannenberg, even the distinctive identity of the three persons is found in their giving of themselves to one another. Generally theologians have distinguished the persons of the Trinity in terms of their relations or their origins. For example, only the Father is unbegotten; only the Son is begotten of the Father; and only the Holy Spirit proceeds from the Father (the Eastern Orthodox view), or from the Father and the Son (the Western Roman Catholic and Protestant view). Pannenberg doesn't deny that the persons can be distinguished on the basis of their origins, but he maintains that their distinctive identities as persons are exhibited *primarily* in their ways of being dependent on one another.[13] Each finds his personhood by being subject to the others and allowing his identity to be established by the others. Theologian Colin

Gunton labels this divine pattern "an ontology of sacrifice" in which "to be is to exist in a dynamic of mutual giving and receiving."[14]

This means that the triune persons are self-actualized not through self-assertion but through self-giving and self-surrender. We tend to view submission or surrender to another as self-limiting and self-destructive—as Much-Afraid first thought about the waterfall flowing onto the rocks below. But in hymnwriter Fanny Crosby's words, as the persons of the Trinity give and receive love from one another, "perfect submission [is] perfect delight." In the fellowship of the Trinity, self-giving and self-sacrifice equals self-fulfillment and unspeakable joy.

THE HEART OF CHRISTIAN LIFE AND MINISTRY

The same holds true for us. Self-giving and self-sacrifice take us not only to the heart of God but to the heart of all creaturely existence as well. In the words of C. S. Lewis:

> For in self-giving, if anywhere, we touch a rhythm not only of all creation but of all being. For the Eternal Word also gives Himself in sacrifice; and that not only on Calvary. . . . From before the foundation of the world He surrenders begotten Deity back to begetting Deity in obedience. . . .
>
> From the highest to the lowest, self exists to be abdicated and, by that abdication, becomes more truly self, to be thereupon yet the more abdicated, and so forever.[15]

When Jesus urged his disciples to lose themselves in order to find themselves (Mark 8:34-35), he was merely telling them to follow the eternal trinitarian pattern embedded in all creation. As bearers of the divine image, we too find our life by losing it. Author Richard Neuhaus expresses it well: "Only when I give up on the search for myself in abandonment to another—to the Other—is my 'I' reconstituted by the 'I' to whom I surrender."[16]

Because self-giving is at the heart of God and all creaturely being, it is also at the heart of Christian ministry. In the New Testament the most commonly used word for ministry clearly conveys this. The Greek words usually rendered in our English translations as "minister" (*diakonos*) and "ministry" (*diakonia*), along with the verb "to minister" (*diakoneo*), are derived from the same *diakoneia* word group that in everyday speech meant "to serve," especially in a personal capacity, and particularly "to wait at table." Our English word *deacon* is derived from these Greek words. By definition, then, ministers, like good restaurant wait staff, are those who focus on the needs and interests of others, not their own.

Jesus defined the purpose of his ministry in these terms. "The Son of Man," he declared, "came not to be ministered unto, but to minister [*diakonein*] and to give his life a ransom for many" (Mark 10:45 KJV). Notice how his ministry and self-giving are bound up together. He also declared that the Son of Man would be glorified by laying down his life, for "unless a grain of wheat falls into the earth and dies, it remains just a single grain; but if it dies, it bears much fruit" (John 12:24). Sacrificial self-giving is thus at the heart of Christ's ministry, and consequently all Christian ministry, which, as I've emphasized before, is a participation in his ongoing ministry.

Unfortunately, many contemporary discussions of ministry fail to adequately emphasize this. As John Stott observes,

> The place of suffering in service and passion in mission is hardly ever taught today. But the greatest single secret of evangelistic or missionary effectiveness is the willingness to suffer and die. It may be a death to popularity (by faithfully preaching the unpopular biblical gospel), or to pride (by the use of modest

methods in reliance on the Holy Spirit), or to racial and national prejudice (by identification with another culture), or to material comfort (by adopting a simple lifestyle). But the servant must suffer . . . to bring light to the nations, and the seed must die if it is to multiply.[17]

Certainly this is a neglected emphasis in current teaching and preparation for ministry, especially in North America. Can you imagine an advertisement in a Christian magazine urging those considering preparation for ministry to choose a particular college or seminary because "we will prepare you to die"? In an age dedicated to self-fulfillment and enamored with success, who wants to hear about sacrifice and self-giving?

Contrast this to the preparation for ministry currently taking place in the underground seminaries of the Chinese house churches. "To escape from the police," a house-church leader told an American pastor, "we teach our students how to jump out of a two-story window so they won't break their legs when they hit the ground." In their seminaries, it is assumed that being in ministry will involve suffering and persecution, perhaps imprisonment and even death.

A century ago, leaders in the Western church were more likely to recognize the crucial place of suffering and self-giving in ministry. Think, for example, of Amy Carmichael, who left England in 1895 to minister to disadvantaged children in south India and remained there until her death in 1951. The title of Elisabeth Elliot's biography of Carmichael sums up her life of joyful self-sacrifice: *A Chance to Die.* Surely this is a crucial dimension of ministry we need to recover today.

DYING TO SELF

Though sacrifice and self-giving in ministry may have been emphasized more in past eras than they are now, because of the nature of human sinfulness they are notions resisted in every age. We often define sin in terms of outward actions contrary to God's law, and certainly Scripture often conceives it that way. For example, 1 John 3:4 states that "everyone who commits sin is guilty of lawlessness; sin is lawlessness." However, lawlessness is not the essence of sin. According to Scripture, sin lies beneath our actions. Sin is ultimately rooted in an inward attitude, a deep-seated self-centeredness, an evil heart out of which sinful actions flow (cf. Mark 7:21-23).

This self-orientation, so deeply entrenched in every one of us, is threatened by sacrificial self-giving and opposes it at all costs. We need, then, to come to terms with our self-centeredness and God's remedy for it before the trinitarian pattern can be realized in our ministry.

The Bible uses several different expressions to describe self-centeredness: the "old self" (Romans 6:6), "the flesh" (Galatians 5:16-17, 24), "the sinful nature" (Romans 7:18, 25 NIV), "the carnal mind" (Romans 8:7; 1 Corinthians 3:1-3 KJV). Essentially it is a self that wants everything and everyone to revolve around it, an ego that puts not God but itself at the center and declares not "Thy will be done" but "My will be done."

Someone once gave Wilfred Grenfell, the great early-twentieth-century medical missionary to Labrador, a powerful new motorboat so he could better navigate among inlets and islands along the coast and respond quickly to those in need. Soon afterward he received an emergency call in the middle of the night from someone who needed immediate medical attention. So he set out in the new boat toward the island where the person lived.

Grenfell knew its location, but in the blackness of the night he was forced to navigate solely by compass. Soon he realized he had embarked in the wrong direction, for when he expected to be nearing the island, no land was in sight. Instead he was heading out into the dangerous open sea, so he reversed the boat and fortunately managed to return home safely.

The next day when Grenfell checked the compass on the boat, he discovered the problem. Whoever had fastened the compass to the boat had run out of brass screws and had used a steel screw to finish the job. That steel screw attracted the magnetic tip of the compass needle to itself. The night before, Grenfell hadn't been charting his course by the magnetic North Pole; instead his compass had been charting its course to itself.

The ego-centeredness, the self-reference, in each of us is like that defective compass. In the Middle Ages, theologians coined a Latin phrase, *cor curvum in se* (curved in on ourselves), to describe it. Because of our bent toward sin, we don't chart our course to do God's will. Self-centeredness and self-interest, the exact opposites of trinitarian self-giving and self-sacrifice, come naturally to us. Hence we seek to promote, protect and preserve ourselves and our interests at all costs.

What happens to this sinful self-orientation when we become Christians? According to the New Testament, at conversion we become new creatures in Christ. The old has passed away and all things have become new (2 Corinthians 5:17). We have been rescued from the kingdom of darkness and transferred to the kingdom of God's Son (Colossians 1:13). Because Jesus is now Lord of our life, we are under new management. In fact, our old self has been crucified with Christ (Romans 6:6). Yet although the old self no longer reigns— Christ does—it is still present and beckons us to walk in the former self-centered way of the flesh instead of the sacrificial, self-giving way of the Spirit (Galatians 5:16-17).

That's why sincere Christians often find themselves living in a state of conflict much like what Paul describes in Romans 7:22-23[18]: "For I delight in the law of God in my inmost self, but I see in my members another law at war with the law of my mind, making me captive to the law of sin that dwells in my members." Caught in a struggle between the new self and the old self, they desire good but are drawn to evil. Like "Mr. Facing-both-ways," the character in John Bunyan's *Pilgrim's Progress*, at times they feel like a walking civil war!

Although they have confessed Jesus as Lord, he is actually more like a houseguest. When you're a houseguest, as I often am when I travel, your hosts will typically say, "Make yourself at home." They are being gracious and hospitable, but you know, of course, there are many things you do in your home that you wouldn't dream of doing as a guest in theirs. For example, you wouldn't insist they change the color of the carpet in the bedroom where you're staying. Nor would you enter their master bedroom to root around in their personal belongings or search their office for their income tax returns. Doing such things would be entirely inappropriate, for it's not your home; you're only a guest there.

Many believers have a relationship with Christ like this. He has brought joy into their home and helped fix up the house. So he is a welcome guest; in fact, they want him to stay permanently. But still they are the owner of the house. Jesus is only a guest.

Jesus is not content to be a guest. He wants to be the president, not just a resident! He wants to exchange places with us so that he's the host and we're the guest. In fact, he wants us to sign over the property deed to him. As Lewis expresses it, "You thought you were going to be made into a decent little cottage: but He is building a palace. He intends to come and live in it Himself."[19]

As Christ begins to challenge us at the point of total ownership or lordship over our life, we often will try to bargain with him by giving him individual rooms, parts of the house but not the whole. We surrender things to him—our time, our money, even our service, yet without surrendering ourselves. We give, sometimes even to great lengths—but we don't give up. As a young American missionary in India put it, "I gave up my homeland, a good job and a good salary to come to India to work for God, but I must admit that I haven't really given myself to him."

Eventually, however, we realize that's exactly what Christ wants from us. As Lewis explains,

> Christ says, "Give me All. I don't want so much of your time and so much of your money and so much of your work: I want You. I have not come to torment your natural self, but to kill it. No half-measures are any good. I don't want to cut off a branch here and a branch there. I want to have the whole tree down. I don't want to drill the tooth, or crown it, or stop it, but to have it out. Hand over the whole natural self, all the desires that you think innocent as well as the ones you think wicked—the whole outfit. I will give you a new self instead. In fact, I will give you Myself: my own will shall become yours."[20]

Inevitably we are brought to a place where Jesus challenges us to surrender ourselves totally to him. We have acknowledged him as Lord, but in reality, although he has come into our life and we have given him certain parts, we're still in charge. Now it's time for his lordship to become actualized in us at a profounder level. We are at a crisis point. We need to undergo a deeper death to self and be brought to a place of full surrender so that Christ can exercise full control.

Mike Breaux, a teaching pastor at Willow Creek Community Church, describes the crucial point in his life like this: "Jesus was an important part of my life, but he was like one spoke of a wheel. There were other spokes too—my ministry, my career, my marriage, my children, my love of sports. But although he was one of the important spokes, I was the hub. Then during a time when I was on a retreat by myself, he confronted me and said, 'Mike, I don't want to just be a spoke. I want to be the hub. I want to be at the center of everything you are and do. Will you turn your life over to me in such a way that I'm the hub?'"[21] Eventually every Christian and everyone in ministry will come to such a crossroads. We have to make a choice: will Christ be the hub or merely a spoke? How we decide will determine the fruitfulness of our life and ministry.

In *They Found the Secret,* first published in 1960, V. Raymond Edman, then president of Wheaton College, presented the lives of twenty well-known late-nineteenth- and early-twentieth-century evangelicals. The list included such spiritual giants as Hudson Taylor, Samuel Logan Brengle, Amy Carmichael, Oswald Chambers, Charles Finney, A. J. Gordon, Dwight L. Moody, Frances Ridley Havergal and Andrew Murray. Though they came from different backgrounds and theological traditions, all went through a profound crisis of self-surrender several years after their conversion—in most cases, after several years of full-time ministry. Only after they had died to self at a deeper level did they enter into the Christ-controlled, Spirit-filled life and ministry they are remembered for.

George Müller, another spiritual giant of that same era, when pressed by someone to divulge the secret of his ministry, said what everyone in Edman's book might have said: "There was a day when I died; utterly died. Died to George Mueller, his opinions, preferences, tastes and will; died to the world, its approval or censure; died to the approval or blame even of my brethren and friends, and, since then, I have studied only to show myself approved unto God."[22] All these persons fully surrendered their right to themselves and were set free from the tyranny of a divided self. Consequently, their lives became a living and holy sacrifice, a fragrant offering, acceptable to God (Romans 12:1), or, to paraphrase Edman's subtitle, "a transformed life that revealed a touch of eternity." Out of their dying to self, they were raised to new life. As they entered deeply into Christ's death, they experienced the power of his resurrection.

Many ministers are willing to follow Christ halfway—but not the other half. They'll give up many things for Christ but will not disown themselves. The women and men in Edman's book found the secret of victory through full surrender. They are examples of what spiritual writer Thomas Kelly describes as "the astonishing life which is willing to follow Him the other half, sincerely to disown itself, this life which intends *complete* obedience, without *any* reservations." Only a few are willing to go the other half, Kelly observes, "but when such a commitment comes in a human life, God breaks through, miracles are wrought, world-renewing divine forces are released, history changes."[23]

Of course, there are misconceptions about full surrender. Like the Pharisee who was proud because he wasn't like the despicable tax collector (Luke 18:9-14), there are those who are proud of their self-surrender. Their self-renunciation is actually an expression of the old self that needs to die! Others get caught in a vicious cycle of trying to make a perfect surrender. Without realizing it, they turn it into a human accomplishment, a way of exalting themselves and their own righteousness. Actually we can no more fully die to ourselves than we can atone for our sins!

What we can do is offer ourselves to God as fully and completely as we know how. Then in response to our surrendered act of will, God will accomplish a deeper work of grace in us, consecrating us completely to his service.

We must also never forget that self-surrender flows out of love. Experiencing the divine embrace, the joyful trinitarian intimacy explored in the last chapter, evokes the response of glad surrender. That's why I discussed it first. When surrender fails to arise out of love, it is of the letter that kills rather than the Spirit that brings life (2 Corinthians 3:6). Remember what the Shepherd says to Much-Afraid at the beginning of her journey: "It is only on the High Places of Love that anyone can receive the power to pour themselves down in an utter abandonment of self-giving."[24]

Some believe that once they have fully surrendered themselves to God, they'll never have to struggle with self-will again. Not so. Jesus himself struggled in the Garden of Gethsemane before he resolved, "Not my will but yours be done" (Luke 22:41-44). As we face new situations, as new issues in life and ministry unfold, we will continue to wrestle with self-will.

Dying to self is therefore both a crisis and a process. I have been underscoring the importance of the crisis aspect, the point at which we say, in the words of the gospel song, "All to Jesus I surrender, all to him I freely give." Having settled that issue once and for all (the crisis), we are then set free to choose the way of surrender and self-giving as we face new situations in life and ministry (the process). In fact, each new circumstance becomes an opportunity to reaffirm our full surrender.

It's like marriage. When we stand at a marriage altar and solemnly vow "I do" and "I will," we really have no idea what those words will mean. Only as each particular situation unfolds do we find out. Yet the commitment established and expressed in our wedding vows remains the indispensable foundation of our marriage. Out of it flow all the particular "I dos" and "I wills" of our married life. Like our wedding vows, our full surrender paves the way for myriad surrenders in the life situations that follow.

That's why despite distortions and misconceptions, self-surrender, as both crisis and process, is absolutely essential for Christian life and ministry. Without it we will never be free to find ourselves by losing ourselves. George Matheson's hymn "Make Me a Captive, Lord" expresses it well:

Make me a captive, Lord, and then I shall be free.
Force me to render up my sword, and I shall conqueror be.
I sink in life's alarms when by myself I stand;
Imprison me within thine arms, and strong shall be my hand.

My will is not my own till thou hast made it thine;
If it would reach a monarch's throne, it must its crown resign.
It only stands unbent amid the clashing strife,
When on thy bosom it has leant, and found in thee its life.[25]

SURRENDER AND SELF-GIVING IN MINISTRY

Full surrender is essential if the trinitarian disposition of self-giving is to take shape in us. When we surrender to God, we are set free to lay ourselves down for others, to choose the way of surrender and self-giving in the particular situations we face in ministry.

What are some of those situations? Obviously the specific circumstances will vary, but as we focus now on the ongoing process of surrender, let's consider two ministry situations in which all of us will be confronted with the need to surrender and die. These are similar to the situations Abraham faced in relation to his two sons, Ishmael and Isaac.

When Abraham first answered God's call, he was promised that he would be the father of a great nation. But ten years later, when Sarah still wasn't pregnant, Abraham became impatient. So when Sarah urged him to sleep with Hagar, her slave girl, he agreed. "God must want to fulfill his promise through her," she said.

It wasn't an indecent proposal. For childless couples at that time, it was a culturally acceptable thing to do. And it did produce results. Abraham slept with Hagar, she conceived, and nine months later Ishmael was born. Abraham finally had a son and an heir of his own flesh and blood. But it wasn't Isaac, the child of promise God had in mind. As Paul sums it up, "The son of Hagar, the slave-wife, was born in a human attempt to bring about the fulfillment of God's promise" (Galatians 4:23 NLT).

We are often tempted to follow the same pattern in our ministry: to bring about God's will and purpose in our own way and in our own strength, according to our own timetable, instead of in God's way and in God's strength, according to God's timetable. Much ministry in the North American church today falls into this category. Rooted in our religious self-determination, done in the power of the flesh, it is a human attempt to accomplish God's will and is descended, therefore, from Ishmael, not Isaac.

Unfortunately, our congregations and even our ecclesiastical superiors often encourage us and reward us for doing it that way. "Be productive," they urge us. "Make it happen." But there is a world of difference between being productive and being fruitful, between striving to build Christ's church and allowing Christ to build his church through you.

I can think back on several times in my ministry when I have yielded to this temptation. Because a certain program or emphasis was currently being used by God in other churches and settings, I insisted on immediately bringing it into mine. Rather than taking the time to bring others on board or to truly contextualize it, in my zeal to see God work through it in my setting as he had elsewhere, I imposed it on others. The result was an Ishmael, not an Isaac.

Henry and Richard Blackaby are right: "Asking God to set one's goals and to bless one's dreams does not ensure that they are from God. Only God can reveal his plans and he does so in his way, on his time schedule, and to whom he wills. How often do Christian leaders claim to have received their vision from God when in fact they have simply dreamed up the most desirable future they could imagine and then prayed for God to bless their efforts as they set out to achieve it?"[26]

Even though God redeemed Abraham and Sarah's mistake by blessing Ishmael, still there was a gut-wrenching day several years after Isaac was born when God said to Abraham, "Get rid of Hagar and Ishmael. Kiss them goodbye. The inheritance belongs to Isaac." And so early one morning Abraham, reluctantly but firmly, sent them away.

There will be painful times of surrender like that in our ministry, when we lay down our attempts to accomplish God's will our way instead of God's way, when we kiss an Ishmael we have concocted goodbye in order to gain an Isaac God has for us.

Eventually Isaac grew into a fine young lad. As Abraham and Sarah watched the child of promise grow, their hearts were knit closer and closer with his. He was the apple of their eye. Their future hopes were pinned on him.

But there came a time when even Isaac, the child of promise, became a problem child—a hindrance to Abraham's relationship with God. For Abraham was delighting more in Isaac, the desire of his heart, than in the Lord (cf. Psalm 37:4). He had made an idol out of Isaac. So one day God said, "Abraham, take your son, your only son Isaac, whom you love, and go and offer him on Mount Moriah as a sacrifice to me."

As in the case of Abraham, often God's best gifts, his children of promise, become more important to us than God himself. God's gifts can usurp the throne of our heart, which only God the Giver is meant to occupy. They become idols we worship instead of him.

That's why God's best gifts must be sacrificed and surrendered back to God to be properly used. So as with Abraham, God will bring us to a Mount Moriah, a place where we have to sacrifice our Isaac, lay down the very best gifts he has given us. Of course, God gave Isaac back to Abraham, and he wants to give our surrendered Isaacs back to us. Having placed them on the altar of sacrifice, we can then love them and use them, no longer in an idolatrous way but in the way God intended all along.

For those of us in Christian ministry, how often our Isaac is our ministry itself. This wonderful gift—the ministry to and for which we have been called, gifted and equipped—can easily become an idol rivaling God. Oswald Chambers's words are penetrating: "The greatest competitor of devotion to Jesus is service for him."[27] Too often we love our ministry more than we love God.

I'll never forget the bitterly cold Sunday morning one February when I realized I had done that. I was alone in the sanctuary of the church I was pastoring, rehearsing the sermon I would preach to the congregation. My words were echoing around, bouncing off the empty pews.

That morning I was preaching on the story we've been exploring here: Abraham and the sacrifice of Isaac. And the gist of my sermon was similar: Like Abraham, we often make idols out of God's best gifts, our Isaacs. So God will call us to surrender them back to him. Then when they've been surrendered and consecrated, he gives them back to us.

But a strange thing happened during that sermon rehearsal. It doesn't happen to preachers very often. I heard my own sermon!

With devastating clarity, I saw what my Isaac was: it was the very ministry God had given me. I had made an idol out of it and was using it to meet my own selfish ego needs, to build my own kingdom as much as Christ's.

I stopped my sermon rehearsal in midsentence and put my head down on the pulpit as tears filled my eyes. "Oh God, forgive me," I cried. "Forgive me for loving my ministry more than you, for finding my joy in my ministry more than in you."

Something inside me died that morning, and from then on ministry was different. There was less drivenness in it and more freedom and joy. It was still mine, but I wasn't clinging to it the way I had been. I was able to hold it lightly, because now I was clinging more to Christ!

Throughout our ministry we will be given countless opportunities to die to ourselves. In such sacrificial self-giving, patterned after the triune self-giving, we find our highest fulfillment, greatest fruitfulness and truest freedom.

Is God calling you to a full surrender of your life and your ministry? Or to a posture of sacrificial self-giving in some specific situation? Listen again and join in the song of the water rushing down from the high places: "*From the heights we leap and flow, To the valleys down below, Sweetest urge and sweetest will, To go lower, lower still.*"

FIVE

COMPLEX SIMPLICITY

The Mystery of Trinitarian Ministry

*The only simplicity to be trusted is the
simplicity to be found on the far side of complexity.*

ALFRED NORTH WHITEHEAD

❖

How can God be three in one? No matter who you are talking to—
a skeptic, a Muslim or a Jew, a child or teenager in Sunday school, an
adult seeker or a mature Christian believer—this question almost always comes up and often dominates discussions about the Trinity.

Of course, it is not the most important question. In fact, framing
the question this way obscures the primary purpose of the doctrine.
Instead of a revelation of God's heart and an invitation to enter into
relationship with the Father, Son and Holy Spirit, when this question
is at the center the Trinity becomes a mathematical problem to be
solved, a doctrine for apologetics to explain and defend, but is of little practical relevance for Christian life and ministry.

Yet still, "How can God be three in one?" is a significant question
because it captures most people's initial reaction to the Trinity. The

Christian formulation that God is one being in three persons and, as Thomas Oden puts it, "neither one nor three without being three in one, yet always one and always three"[1] is counterintuitive. It seems illogical and irrational. In a word, it's mystifying.

Christians have always used various analogies to help make sense of the Trinity. Water, for example, can exist in three different states, as liquid, steam or ice. It is one substance (H_2O) yet appears in three distinct forms. A tree exists as root, trunk and branches; a candle as wax, wick and flame; an egg as white, yolk and shell.

In a children's sermon a pastor used an apple to explain the Trinity. With a sharp knife he cut a shiny red apple in half to reveal its three parts to the children: the peel, the flesh and the core. All three are apple, he stressed. The peel is apple, the flesh is apple, and the core is apple. But they are also different. The peel is not the flesh; the flesh is not the core; the core is not the peel. No one part is the other two. Yet although they're different, they are all apple, and there is only one apple.

God is like this apple, he told the children. God is one being but consists of three distinct persons, Father, Son and Holy Spirit. Like the three parts of the apple, the Father is God, the Son is God, and the Holy Spirit is God. Yet there is one God.

Such analogies for the Trinity do have their place. In his great fifth-century work *On the Trinity,* Augustine reasoned that since God has left his imprint on his creation and humans were created in God's image, we should expect to find traces of the Trinity in the creation and ourselves. Augustine is especially known for his psychological analogy, which posits a reflection of the Trinity in the mind's act of knowing, which involves memory, understanding and will.

However, trinitarian analogies are of limited use, and eventually all break down. Augustine himself was careful to emphasize this. Beware, he warned, of thinking that these analogies "are in any sort to be equaled with the Holy Trinity, to be squared after an analogy; that is, a kind of exact rule of comparison."[2] When pressed, every analogy for the Trinity results in *tritheism* (that God exists as three separate and independent persons, Father, Son and Holy Spirit) or *modalism* (that God manifests himself at different times as a different person, first as Father, then as Son, then as Holy Spirit, but that God is not eternally three persons), heresies the church has always rejected.

The point is, in spite of our best efforts to understand and explain it, the Trinity will always remain a mystery. Although it's not an irrational or illogical belief, it transcends human reason. Our minds are incapable of fully grasping it because it is beyond their comprehension.

In his discussion of the Trinity in *Mere Christianity*, C. S. Lewis draws on the story of the "Flatlanders," who live in a two-dimensional world, to illustrate our predicament with regard to the Trinity. The Flatlanders can conceive of lines and fields but not depths and cubes. Likewise, because we are limited to three dimensions (four if we include time), we can't conceive how God can be perfectly One yet three distinct persons.[3] We simply don't have access to all the dimensions God inhabits. Someday when we see face to face (1 Corinthians 13:12) we will understand more fully. For now, from our limited three-dimensional perspective, we see through a glass darkly.

As the church father Gregory Nazianzen says, we are "blinded by the light of the Trinity." Writing in the fourth century, he expressed what many have experienced in contemplating it: "No sooner do I conceive of the One than I am illumined by the Splendor of the Three; no sooner do I distinguish Them than I am carried back to the One. When I think of any One of the Three I think of Him as the Whole, and my eyes are filled, and the greater part of what I am thinking of escapes me."[4] Just as for Gregory, reflecting deeply on the Trinity makes our minds reel. It has a dizzying effect on us. We are mystified.

Yet given who God is and who we are, isn't this exactly as it should be? After Paul has grappled with the mystery of God's purposes with Israel, he joyfully exclaims: "O the depth of the riches and wisdom and knowledge of God! How unsearchable are his judgments and how inscrutable his ways!" (Romans 11:33). Paul's inability to penetrate the mystery evokes exhilaration and wonder in him, not confusion and frustration.

This is an important function of the doctrine of the Trinity. Gerhard Tersteegen, the eighteenth-century German mystic, was right: "a God understood, a God comprehended, is no God."[5] The Trinity, then, safeguards and secures the mystery of God. It establishes and affirms, as Paul declares in 1 Timothy 3:16, that "without any doubt, the mystery of our religion is great."

In contemplating the mystery of the Trinity—the subject of this chapter—we will consider three related concepts that are foundational for a Christian worldview and have important implications for the vocation of ministry:

1. *Mystery.* The Trinity not only establishes the mystery of God but also points to the element of mystery in all existence. Yet what exactly does divine mystery entail, and how should it shape our approach to ministry?

2. *Paradox.* The doctrine of the Trinity presents us with two seemingly logically incompatible statements: God is one being; God is three persons. And God is never one without being three or three without being one. To speak the truth about God we must affirm both. This is the first of many paradoxes we encounter in the Christian faith. How then do we handle paradox in the practice of ministry?

3. *Simplicity.* The fact that we can distinguish the persons of the Trin-

ity doesn't mean there are three gods. God is Three-in-*One*. There is only one God. For God is simple, one with himself, and cannot be divided into parts. As Thomas Oden states, "God's unity is not a unity of separable parts but of distinguishable persons."[6] Yet *tri-unity* indicates that divine unity is not absolutely undifferentiated unity but differentiated unity. The divine simplicity is therefore not simplistic but a complex simplicity. What then does this reveal about the nature of things, and how should it inform ministry?

Mystery, paradox, simplicity—these three general concepts are more abstract than and perhaps not as implicit in the doctrine of the Trinity as the other six characteristics of trinitarian life. Some might contend that any religious teacher or philosopher could affirm these general concepts, whether they are Christian or not. Of course you don't have to believe in the Trinity to affirm these concepts, but for Christians who do, they are related—if not directly at least indirectly—to belief in the triune God and have important implications for ministry.

EMBRACING MYSTERY

According to the *Catechism of the Catholic Church,* "The Trinity is the central mystery of the Christian faith and life. It is the source of all other mysteries of Christian Faith, the light that enlightens them."[7] More than any other Christian doctrine, the Trinity sets before us the mystery of God and points to the element of mystery in every aspect of our faith.

As I've already noted, this is a good thing. The Trinity reminds us that our highest reasoning powers and most profound logical categories will never penetrate or fully comprehend, explain or contain, resolve or remove the mystery of God. Our finest words about God are but feeble, faltering attempts to express what can never fully or adequately be conveyed in any human language.

When we forget this, we are apt to become smug and self-satisfied, narrow-minded and intolerant, as if somehow we have a corner on the truth, a knowledge of God superior to all others. So we need to be reminded that God can't be completely contained and imprisoned in any of our categories. He breaks out of all our carefully constructed boxes.

Earlier I mentioned Augustine's monumental *On the Trinity,* which he worked on for fifteen years. Shortly after he had completed it, he was walking along the Mediterranean shore on the coast of North Africa when he chanced upon a boy who kept filling a bucket with seawater and pouring it into a large hole in the sand.

"Why are you doing that?" Augustine asked the boy.

"I'm pouring the Mediterranean Sea into the hole," the boy replied in all seriousness.

"My dear boy, what an impossible thing to try to do!" chided Augustine. "The sea is far too vast, and your hole is far too small."

Then as Augustine continued his walk, it dawned on him that in his efforts to write on the Trinity he was much like that boy: the subject was far too vast, and his mind was far too small!

The Trinity establishes and proclaims the mystery of God; it reminds us that we cannot fully fathom the unfathomable. In life and ministry it is important to learn what we *cannot* know. The Trinity teaches us to acknowledge and embrace the limits of our knowledge.

Our modern scientific mindset has little time or patience with mystery. We pride ourselves in being able to penetrate the unknown and offer solutions to life's most perplexing problems. No doubt as a result of modern science we have taken giant strides forward in uncovering knowledge about our world and overcoming superstition.

But science has also fostered the false assumption that given enough study and research, we can figure anything out.

When people impatient with mystery show up in church, they put pressure on those of us in ministry to dispense with it. "Give us quick and easy answers for faith's deepest questions," they insist. "Isn't that what you've been trained to do and what we pay you to do?"

The Trinity, however, forces us to acknowledge that not only are there things we don't know now but there are some things we will never know. Who wants to be told that? It's disconcerting and unsettling; it makes us feel out of control. It is tempting, then, for those of us in ministry to avoid mystery ourselves and to help others avoid it. As A. W. Tozer suggests, "To admit that there is One who lies beyond us, who exists outside of all our categories, who will not be dismissed with a name, who will not appear before the bar of our reason, nor submit to our curious inquiries: this requires a great deal of humility, more than most of us possess, so we save face by thinking God down to our level, or at least down to where we can manage Him."[8]

Tozer also discerns the deeper intent of the mystery of the Trinity. By confronting us with the limits of our knowledge, it bids us to bow in reverence and to assume a posture of humble adoration. The verse of a hymn captures it well:

Holy Father, Holy Son,
Holy Spirit;
Three we name Thee;
while in essence only one,
Undivided God we claim thee;
And adoring bend the knee,
While we own the Mystery.[9]

In the presence of this mystery, we are no longer in a position of control where we can manage or master the subject. Before this Subject, worship is more appropriate than problem solving, awe is preferable to answers. So the mystery of the Trinity ought to evoke in us humility and worship—the very attitudes necessary for entering the circle of triune fellowship.

We must be clear, however, that the mystery of the Trinity does *not* mean we know nothing definitive about God since "it's all a mystery." Understanding the meaning of the Greek word *mysterion* used by the New Testament writers can help us here. Although our English word *mystery* is derived from this word, its popular meaning today is significantly different from its meaning in the original Greek.

In current English, a mystery is something obscure, dark, secret or puzzling, like a murder mystery. If something is "mysterious," it's inexplicable, incomprehensible and enigmatic. The Greek word as used by the New Testament writers, however, has a distinctively different meaning. Instead of an impenetrable unlocked secret, it points to an *open* secret, one that has been revealed.

The Trinity, then, like all the mysteries of the Christian faith, is a truth beyond human discovery. We didn't come up with it on our own. We know it only because God has taken the initiative and revealed it to us. Because God himself "has spoken to us by a Son" (Hebrews 1:2), Christians believe we have been given definitive knowledge of God. So we confidently proclaim that God as Father, Son and Holy Spirit is Three in One and One in Three.

Our definitive knowledge of God, however, is not exhaustive. As we *apprehend* God's triune self-revelation, we also acknowledge and gladly confess that we do not fully *comprehend* God. We are grateful that God has revealed himself to us, but we also recognize that the greater whole eludes our grasp. Thus God's self-revelation dissolves divine mystery and preserves it at the same time.

Augustine worked hard to understand the revelation that God is Three in One. In constructing a doctrine of the Trinity, he developed a precise and elaborate technical vocabulary. Yet he never entertained illusions about his ability to penetrate the mystery of the Trinity. As he said, he developed his vocabulary "not that [the mystery] might be spoken, but that it not be left unspoken."[10] In the twentieth century, Roman Catholic theologian Karl Rahner echoed what Augustine and all the great theologians have understood: the Trinity "is an absolute mystery which we do not understand even after it has been revealed."[11] Thus the mystery always remains. Our best thinking doesn't dispel the mystery but actually deepens it.

Yet as an open secret, the nature of the mystery has been transformed. The *revealed* mystery, in contrast to a hidden mystery, is the mystery of light, not darkness, the mystery of the known, not the unknown. As Eugene Peterson points out, in the New Testament mystery is "not the mystery of a darkness that must be dispelled but the mystery of a light that may be entered. It is not something we don't know but something that is too much to know."[12]

How should this understanding of the mystery of the Trinity inform our understanding of ministry? In an age that wants to reduce everything to a problem to be solved, it is tempting to approach ministry that way. Ministry then becomes all about what we can do to figure out and fix things. Of course, there is an important place for figuring and fixing in ministry, but as Peterson maintains, "if that's all we do we become myopic, managers and mechanics of what is immediately before us, with no peripheral vision and no horizons. We miss most of life."[13]

Approaching life and ministry as a mystery to be entered instead of a problem to be solved opens us to hidden meanings, depths that are beyond our categories and calculations. Even after we have exerted our best efforts and skills, there is always more in any situation than we can comprehend. Knowing that frees us from having to figure everything out, to have all the answers and to always be in control. Instead of frustrating us, the presence of mystery evokes gratitude, for it is the gateway to humility and wonder.

Time and again as I have engaged in the ministry of healing prayer, I have found myself in the presence of mystery. There is the mystery of suffering and evil. "How could so-and-so do such an awful thing to me, and why did God allow it to happen?" I am often asked. And I humbly admit that I don't really have a satisfactory answer. Then there is the mystery of the way healing unfolds in a person's life. Christ's healing power sometimes manifests itself in dramatic, miraculous ways and there are major breakthroughs. At other times, however, healing comes through a difficult, drawn-out, deliberate process in which every three steps forward are followed by two steps backward. On some occasions, then, I find myself praying boldly and authoritatively; on others I can only encourage someone to hang on even when God seems absent. Finally, there is the mystery of God's strength being made perfect in weakness. That which brought evil into someone's life is transformed into an instrument for good. What was once a cause of brokenness becomes a means of conveying Christ's fullness. In wonder and gratitude I exclaim, "Lord, what an amazing thing you have done!"

LIVING WITH PARADOX

God is one being; God is three persons. To speak the truth about God we must assert both of these seemingly incompatible, contradictory assertions. We can never simply assert one or the other, or stress one to the neglect of the other. Thus the Trinity presents us with an antinomy or a dialectical contradiction, or—the term that I prefer—a paradox.

We have already stressed that God cannot be comprehended in human words and categories. Our minds simply aren't adequate for the task. Consequently, the best way to express God's self-revelation in words is through paradox. Theologian D. M. Baillie suggests it's like drawing a map of our spherical world on the page of an atlas. There will always be a certain degree of falsification, because, as in Lewis's "Flatlander" illustration, the two-dimensional surface is incapable of adequately representing our three-dimensional world. Does this mean we should dispense with maps and atlases? Of course not. In our spherical world, they are necessary and helpful.

A good atlas, however, recognizes this limitation. So to help us overcome it, the atlas offers two different maps of the world to compare with each other. As Baillie describes it, "The one is contained in two circles representing two hemispheres. The other is contained in an oblong (Mercator's projection). Each is a map of the whole world, and they contradict each other to some extent at every point. Yet they are both needed, and taken together they correct each other."[14]

As in the case of all the paradoxes of the Christian faith, so it is with the Trinity: the paradox is necessary, not because God is self-contradictory but because our limited minds are inadequate to describe the triune God. The best we can do is speak in paradox: God is one being; God is three persons. The two assertions seem to logically contradict each other, but like the two maps in the atlas, taken together they correct each other and contribute to our better grasp of the truth.

Of course, there is a place where the apparent contradiction is resolved. However, it is in the realm of faith and religious experience, not in the realm of strict logic. Like the circle and the oblong in the atlas, these two-dimensional depictions of a three-dimensional sphere will always appear contradictory. They need to be in order to best represent the three-dimensional reality. But when we look at them, is the fact that they logically appear to be contradictory cause for alarm? Does it make us feel as if we live in an irrational, schizophrenic world? Of course not. It doesn't concern us because we view the two maps in the light of our life in a three-dimensional spherical world. There, in our three-dimensional experience of the world, the apparent two-dimensional logical contradiction is resolved.

So it is with the Trinity, as well as the other Christian paradoxes. In the realm of theology, where we engage in rational reflection on our faith, there will always remain an element of logical contradiction. The contradiction is resolved, however, in the realm of religious experience. In our experience of God, where we both personally and corporately enter the fellowship of the Trinity, the fact that God is three in one makes perfect sense, and there is no contradiction at all.

Some, however, insist on trying to resolve it in the realm of strict logic too, by emphasizing one side of the paradox at the expense of the other. This is one of the main reasons theological heresies spring up. By elevating one side of the paradox and downplaying the other, at first glance, heresies seem to make more sense than the orthodox view that insists on emphasizing both. That's why heresies are appealing and attractive. Their oversimplifications may initially appear more plain and logical, but in the end they prove less true. The half-truth they would have us believe, disconnected from the other half, results in a whole lie. That's what theological error most often is: not the absence of truth, but truth separated from its balancing counterpart. It's attractive because often it is easier to go to a logical extreme than to live in the tension of biblical paradox.

In Paul's willingness to live in such tension, he is an instructive example for us. According to Gordon Fee, in his paradoxical understanding of Christian existence Paul lived in "the radical middle," affirming two seemingly incompatible ideas. On the one hand, he believed that since Jesus had been raised and the Holy Spirit poured out, the future age to come is already a reality in our present age. Hence we are living in the "last days" and experience the presence of the future now. On the other hand, Paul believed that the continued presence of evil, suffering and brokenness in this present age indicates that the future age is also still to come and will be fully realized only when Christ returns. So he lived in "the radical middle" between the beginning of the end and the consummation of the end, insisting that the future is both here (already) and not fully here (not yet).

His understanding of the work of the Holy Spirit—something that often divides Christians today—is similarly in the radical middle. Paul regularly expected to see miraculous demonstrations of the Spirit, but he also stressed that the Spirit's power is often manifested in weakness. As Fee says, "Power [is] sometimes attested by signs and wonders and at other times by joy in great affliction."[15] Today we have groups in the church that traditionally emphasize one or the other, but miss the radical middle of Paul and the New Testament.

In our ministries, the radical middle of affirming both sides of the paradox often eludes us too. I could cite many examples, but I want to focus on one related to the paradoxical nature of the church with which almost everyone in ministry must contend. Chapter two referred to Christian Schwarz's comprehensive study (one thousand churches in thirty-two countries) of healthy, growing churches. His concept of "natural church development" and especially the eight characteristics of healthy churches (empowering leadership, gift-oriented ministry, passionate spirituality, functional structures, inspiring worship services, holistic small groups, need-oriented evangelism and loving relationships) have helped scores of churches worldwide to evaluate themselves and enhance their ministries.

Yet having interviewed hundreds of Christian leaders, Schwarz is convinced that "the greatest obstacle to strategic church development is not a lack of awareness of these characteristics or methodological know-how, but deep-rooted theological blockages."[16] By "theological blockages" Schwarz doesn't mean an adherence to false doctrine but an inability to grasp "the bipolar nature of the church" as both an "organism" (the dynamic pole) and an "organization" (the static pole).

The New Testament, he points out, uses biological, organic metaphors to emphasize the one and architectural, technical metaphors to emphasize the other. In fact, there are points where "the two aspects are so closely intertwined in a single statement that the resulting picture—judged by standards of linear logic—seems contradictory."[17] As examples, Schwarz cites phrases such as "living stones" (1 Peter 2:4-8) and "growing into a temple" (Ephesians 2:19-22), the description of the Corinthians as "God's field and God's building" (1 Corinthians 3:9), and the body of Christ as both growing and being built up (Ephesians 4:12, 16).

Many Christian leaders fail to live in the radical middle of this bipolar paradigm and operate out of either an "institutionalistic" or a "spiritualistic" paradigm, says Schwarz. The institutionalistic paradigm leans toward the right, equating the true church with external institutional structures. The spiritualistic paradigm, by contrast, leans toward the left and is anti-institutional through and through.[18]

Schwarz says that when he presents his material on natural church development, based on the bipolar, paradoxical understanding of the church as both organism and organization, ministers often misinterpret it because they are situated on the right or the left, not in the radical middle where both sides of the paradox are adequately affirmed. "Whereas representatives of the institutional paradigm largely misunderstand these resources in a technocratic way and—in spite of a well-rehearsed litany of denying it—attempt to *make* the church grow, spiritualists tend to pick out those elements that emphasize spirituality and redefine them in a spiritualistic way . . . as an internal, spiritual growth."[19]

Schwarz is thankful for those he has encountered who are able to affirm both sides of the paradox. He describes one such person, a pastor of a church in Switzerland:

> When you are sitting with him, you get the impression that nothing in the world is more important for him than the individual. He says that the entire ministry, both personal and corporate, is built on relationships. He takes much time to form friendships with the members of his leadership team. He places great emphasis on counseling. When he is leading a church service, he is keen that the Holy Spirit should be actively present and able to work in ways that transcend all human planning. And everything must happen with much love.
>
> But this is not all we can say about him. The very same person who is so keen on relationships with individuals can also get enthusiastic about plans and organizational structures. [He] is a sober, calculating strategist. In each of his decisions he rationally considers what the outcome will be. When he thinks through alternative solutions to a problem, a whole sequence of scenarios with consequences for each possible decision goes through his mind.
>
> The characteristic element of people like [him] is that these two poles are not seen as a contradiction. [He] is not a schizophrenic who sometimes plays one role and sometimes the other, and who changes personality whenever he switches roles (although people who regard the two poles as contradictory may perceive it that way).[20]

Have you learned to live in the radical middle in relation to the paradox of the bipolar nature of the church? Or do you operate from an institutionalistic or spiritualistic paradigm? The doctrine of the Trinity, with its seeming logical contradiction that God is one being in three persons, invites those of us in ministry not to resolve the tension but to live with paradox and chart our course toward the radical middle.

COMPLEX SIMPLICITY

When we first conceive of a perfect unity, we often describe it in mathematical terms, in which the ultimate criterion for unity is the absence of multiplicity. If we restrict our thinking to the mathematical model, 1 is 1, 3 is 3, 1 is not 3, and 3 is not 1. Within this framework, the Trinity becomes problematic because it creates a mathematical conundrum.

Yet as theologian Leonard Hodgson points out, most of us are also well acquainted with unities that are not so simple. For example, there is the unity of a work of art or the unity of a living creature. In contrast to mathematical unities, these organic unities, as Hodgson calls them, "can only exist at all by virtue of the presence of . . . the multiplicity of the varied elements which constitute the work of art or the living creature."[21] Here, in contrast to mathematics, unity doesn't preclude multiplicity but presumes it. In fact, the higher the entity, the more complex the unity in multiplicity becomes.

So it is with the unity of the Trinity. As theologian Clark Pinnock suggests, "Unity is not a simple idea. Unity can admit of great complexity. . . . Trinity is a mystery, but it is not an irrationality. It epitomizes the complexity in unity that we find everywhere in experience."[22] God is simple, one with himself, and therefore cannot be divided into parts; yet God is three divine persons in one being. *Tri-*

unity means that divine unity is not absolutely undifferentiated unity but differentiated unity, not the simplistic unity of mathematical integers but the complex unity of divine persons. The divine simplicity is not a simplistic but a complex simplicity.

Since God's nature is reflected in the world he has made, we should expect to find intimations of the Trinity in creaturely existence, and indeed we do. In relation to the main issues of life and ministry, we therefore discover another paradox: *nothing is so simple that it's not also complex, and nothing is so complex that it's not also simple.* There is a complex simplicity and a simple complexity built into the nature of things.

Nothing is so simple that it's not also complex. What does this mean for ministry? There has always been a temptation to evade complexity in ministry by reducing it to formulas, programs, technologies and quick fixes. Moses succumbed to it when, instead of carefully following God's directions, he struck the rock rather than speaking to it. He had struck a rock once before and water had poured forth, so he assumed it would work again (Numbers 20:2-12). Jesus resisted the temptation when Satan urged him to instantly prove he was the Son of God by jumping down from the pinnacle of the temple (Matthew 4:5-7).

I'll never forget the tearful sharing of a forty-year-old man in a Sunday school class. When he was thirteen years old, his beloved elderly grandfather was critically ill. For days the boy prayed earnestly that God would heal him. Eventually, however, his grandfather died, and the boy began to grieve deeply. Unfortunately, his pastor made him feel even worse. "If you had only had faith," he said emphatically, "God would have healed your grandfather."

"In my mind I know it's not true," the man told the class. "But ever since that time, I've felt like I was responsible for my grandfather's death, and I still feel guilty about it."

What deadly fruit his pastor's simplistic understanding of the role of faith in healing had borne in this man's life. Having been engaged in healing ministry for years, I've come to believe that it's more complex than that. Following Ken Blue's insightful discussion in his excellent book *Authority to Heal*,[23] I would state it like this: There is no strict cause-and-effect relationship between faith and healing; nevertheless, expectant faith is often a crucial factor in healing.

I could go on to explain that statement, but here I want only to make the point this case illustrates: the simplicity of ministry, in keeping with God's triune nature, is a complex simplicity. As the philosopher Alfred North Whitehead puts it, "The only simplicity to be trusted is the simplicity to be found on the far side of complexity."[24] Ministry therefore cannot be reduced to sound bites, programs, technologies, tidy formulas and quick fixes.

Soon after graduating from seminary, David Hansen realized this while pastoring several small churches in rural Montana:

> When I began pastoral ministry, I had lots of books prescribing pastoral ministry—the so-called how-to books. I had books on how to preach, how to administrate a church, how to do pastoral counseling and how to lead small groups. They didn't help me. The authors assumed too much. They assumed that I knew what my goal was. They assumed that I knew what I was and who I was. They assumed that I knew why I was supposed to be doing the things they were teaching me about. But I didn't know what I was, or who I was, or why I was supposed to be doing the things I was supposed to be doing. And I didn't know how any of the things I was supposed to be doing fit into a coherent understanding of my call from God to be a pastor.[25]

The problem with how-to books, Hansen concluded, was that they reduce ministry to a technology. On one level they were helpful, since he needed to acquire certain skills and receive good practical advice. But much more than the tasks he carried out, his life as a pastor was a calling encompassing his entire life.

For helping him integrate his life with his work, he found reading books from the classical disciplines of theology more helpful than how-to books. And most helpful were the biographies of well-known pastors and fictional accounts involving pastors. "The stories I read helped me to understand my life comprehensively. My life, too, is a story, and it is the narrative quality of my life that makes my ministry happen."[26]

Our pragmatic age wants to reduce everything to function and technology; the three-in-one unity of the Trinity warns us that it's not that simple. In ministry, nothing is so simple it's not also complex.

At the same time, nothing is so complex that it's not also simple. The antidote to the reductionistic "simplistic simplicity" in ministry I have been disparaging is not a complex complexity in which everything is tenuous, ambiguous and unsettled. Recognizing that we don't have all the answers doesn't mean we never have *any*. Having eschewed a simplicity "on the near side of complexity," I would agree with Whitehead that there is a simplicity "on the far side of complexity."

When I teach basic Christian theology to seminary students and we study the person and work of Christ, we usually examine the four great christological councils, beginning with Nicaea in 325, followed by Constantinople in 381 and Ephesus in 431, and culminating with Chalcedon in 451. For over 125 years the church critically wrestled with various issues related to the person of Christ. Arius, Appolinarius, Nestorius and others set forth positions that were rejected. There were personal and political rivalries between bishops and regions, cultural differences between East and West, translation problems between Greek and Latin. It was a long, drawn-out complex process. The orthodox understanding of the person of Christ wasn't arrived at overnight.

Yet when the whole church finally affirmed the definitive Chalcedonian Creed in 451, it could be summed up in one simple sentence: Jesus Christ is truly God, truly human and truly one. What had seemed at times so elusive and complex had become simple again. And because it was a simplicity arrived at on the far side of complexity, in its richness, power and depth it has stood the test of time.

Something similar happens in the practice of ministry. Take preaching. We may begin with an overly simplistic approach based on sermons we have heard and the few we have preached. Then we take a course in homiletics and discover how complex it is! Preaching, we come to realize, is both an art and a science. There are scores of helpful books advocating different approaches to sermon preparation and delivery. There are model sermons by great preachers that make us wonder if we'll ever preach anything worthwhile.

After we have passed the homiletics course and graduated from school, we are called or sent to pastor a local congregation where we are expected to preach weekly. Aware of our inadequacy for the complexity and immensity of the task, we approach it with fear and trembling.

But several years later, having prepared and delivered a few hundred sermons and preached enough to develop our own style, we reach a point on the far side of complexity where preaching has become simple again. We still approach it with fear and trembling, but also with confidence and joy.

We go through a similar process in relation to many aspects of ministry. The philosopher Paul Ricoeur coined a phrase, "second naiveté," that is apropos. There is a childish, uncritical first naiveté, Ricoeur says, that we need to outgrow. To move beyond it, we must question our assumptions, dissect them and take them apart. In doing so we realize how naive we were and how complex things are.

But the purpose of this deconstruction stage is not to leave us tentative and unsure about everything. Ultimately it should lead to a second naiveté, an understanding arrived at on the far side of complexity, which is truly childlike as opposed to childish. As Richard John Neuhaus explains it, "Having come to recognize that things could theoretically be other than they are, we are brought to the perception that they are as we thought them to be, but on the far side of all our questioning, we *know* that in a way we did not know it before."[27]

The complex simplicity of the Trinity thus points to what we often encounter in the vocation and practice of ministry: nothing is so complex that it's not also simple. The lines by T. S. Eliot capture it well:

We shall not cease from exploration
And the end of all our exploring
Will be to arrive where we started
And know the place for the first time.[28]

GRACIOUS SELF-ACCEPTANCE

The Particularity of Trinitarian Ministry

Be who you is, because if you is who you ain't, you ain't who you is.

LARRY HEIN

❊

Harold Turner, an authority on world religions and emerging religious movements in primitive societies, maintains that essentially there are only three major worldviews: the atomic, the oceanic and the relational. The atomic, symbolized by a group of billiard balls, sees reality in terms of distinct individual units. Here the individual person as an autonomous center of knowing and willing is the ultimate constituent of society. The individualism prevalent in contemporary Western culture reflects the atomic view.

In the oceanic worldview, symbolized by the ocean, the whole is ultimate, not the individual parts. As raindrops falling onto the surface of the ocean lose their particular identity, so ultimately everything will be merged into one identity, which is the soul of all that exists. This is the worldview of Hinduism and many Eastern religions.

A net made up of distinct yet connected strands of rope symbolizes the third major worldview, the relational. This view, which sees everything in the material world and human society constituted by relationship, characterizes primitive societies and primal religions. I is also the worldview closest to the Bible and our trinitarian faith. Rooted in an understanding of God as Three-in-One, it stands dis tinctly apart from the atomic and oceanic views.

Earlier we considered how the trinitarian understanding of persons differs from the atomic, typically reflected in Western individualism where persons are viewed as self-contained, self-reliant individuals. In stead of defining personhood primarily in terms of separateness from others, the trinitarian view defines it in terms of relations. The Father, Son and Holy Spirit each find their distinct identity in their relationships with each other. In fact, they cannot exist as persons apart from each other. Personhood is therefore freedom *for,* not freedom *from,* another.

Yet for all its emphasis on the relational nature of persons, the trinitarian perspective, in contrast to the oceanic, never envisions a time when the three persons of the Trinity will be merged into one. The unity of the Trinity, as noted in the last chapter, is differentiated, not absolute. There will always be three divine persons. The relational distinctions between the Father, Son and Holy Spirit are eternal, not temporary.

This characteristic of the Trinity, particularity or otherness as it is commonly called, has significant implications for Christian faith and practice as well as the vocation of ministry.

TRINITARIAN PARTICULARITY

In the Trinity, according to Orthodox theologian John Zizoulas, there is "a reality of communion in which each particular is affirmed as *unique* and irreplaceable by the others."[1] Thus the Father, Son and Holy Spirit always remain distinct and should never be confused with each other. In their eternal, face-to-face communion, they delight in the otherness of each other.

Theologians accentuate the particular identities of the trinitarian persons in several ways. One is to point out the unique source of each. Of the three persons, the Father alone is unoriginated or unbegotten, having no source other than himself. The Son, on the other hand, is begotten or generated from the Father, while the Holy Spirit, in distinction from the Son, proceeds or is breathed from the Father. In the eighth century, John of Damascus, another Orthodox theologian, expressed it well:

> For the Father is without cause and unborn; for He is derived from nothing, but derives from Himself His being, nor does He derive a single quality from another. Rather He is Himself the beginning and cause of the existence of all things in a definite and natural manner. But the Son is derived from the Father after the manner of generation, and the Holy Spirit likewise is derived from the Father, yet not after the manner of generation, but after that of procession. And we have learned that there is a difference between generation and procession, but the nature of that difference we in no wise understand.[2]

Concerning the generation of the Son from the Father and the procession of the Holy Spirit from the Father, John acknowledges that although there is a difference, we don't know what it is! So why make the distinction at all? Because Scripture uses these different words to describe the origin of the Son (John 1:14, 18) and the Holy Spirit (John 15:26), and it helps us distinguish them from each other.

Another way theologians indicate the differences between the triune persons is by stressing their different functions or actions toward the world. Traditionally God's works, or actions of God in relation to the world, have been categorized under three main headings: creation, redemption and sanctification. Of course, because God is one, the Father, Son and Holy Spirit always act in concert and play a part in all these acts. According to Scripture, they all create (Psalm 33:6-9; John 1:3; Genesis 1:2), redeem (Acts 2:24; John 5:21; Romans 1:4) and sanctify (1 Thessalonians 5:23; Ephesians 5:26; 1 Peter 1:2).

Yet Scripture also assigns the primary role in each of these actions to a different member of the Trinity. Theologians call this the doctrine of *appropriations*. As David Cunningham explains, "We 'appropriate' a particular activity to one of the Three, in order that we might better understand its role in the overall divine plan, and thereby grow closer to God."[3] Thus the Father is the primary actor in creation, the Son in redemption and the Holy Spirit in sanctification. Each person has a locus of work and responsibility and a distinctive function, although it is certainly not an absolute division of labor.

Finally, theologians underscore the distinctions between the trinitarian persons by using different prepositions to characterize their distinctive roles in the divine-human relationship. For example, in describing the role of each of the triune persons in God's saving actions, we say that salvation is *from* the Father, *through* the Son and *by* the Holy Spirit. Our response to what God has done, whether it involves repentance, prayer, gratitude, obedience or worship, is also trinitarian in nature: *by* the Spirit, *through* the Son and *to* the Father.

Of course, the distinctions between the Father, Son and Holy Spirit must always be viewed in the context of their relationships and interactions with each other. The three persons are not private, isolated individuals. In the Trinity, otherness and relation go together. Personal identity is constituted in a network of relationships, so that there is uniqueness without individualism. Cunningham sums it up well: "Because God is Three, particularity is necessarily a trinitarian virtue; and yet, because God is also One, we are called to construe this particularity in an anti-individualistic way."[4]

Understood in this manner, trinitarian particularity or otherness has important implications for the Christian worldview and the Christian understanding of persons. Earlier we maintained that human personhood, modeled after the Trinity, is essentially relational. To *be* is to *be in relationship*. Now, again based on the Trinity, we must also maintain that particularity or otherness is essential to personhood.

Being a person, then, is not simply being a part of a greater whole, existing only for the collective or the nation. In the final scheme of things, when God's purpose for creation and humanity is fully realized, we will not, as Richard Neuhaus puts it, "lose ourselves in a great tapioca pudding of homogeneity."[5] To be a person is to be uniquely who we are and distinct from others. It is our glory—not an unfortunate accident or a temporary arrangement—that we are other, each unique and different. As the poet William Wordsworth expresses it, all persons "differ, by mystery not to be explained."[6]

Among contemporary trinitarian theologians, Colin Gunton has especially emphasized this aspect of personhood. He is concerned that although the modern market economy publicly extols the virtues of pluralism, there are forces at work within it seeking to merge us into one:

> For all its apparent pluralism, the world of the market that so dominates our lives is actually working to make us all identical: all to drink Coca Cola and to eat at McDonald's, those symbols of the homogenizing forces of modernity, all to wear the same only superficially different designer clothes. That is simply another way of swallowing us up into a whole, of effectively depriving us of our individuality. Personal being is precisely at stake in this modern world. Wherever we look, the many—particular people with all their differences—are depersonalized by being swallowed up into the one, the mass,

where individuality is suppressed in the interest of efficiency economics and homogeneity: where babies with a risk of handicap are killed in the womb because we don't want to bother with those who are different, and where all have cosmetic surgery so that we look alike. . . .

Over against this, the triune God is a God in whom the one is not played against the many, nor the many against the one.[7]

Along with the loss of the particularity of human persons in the modern world, Gunton sees a corresponding loss of "an adequate conception of the concreteness of the world in which personal life is lived."[8] In contrast, a trinitarian perspective causes us to value the particulars of the material world—cabbages and mountains, insects and rocks, songs and statues in all their concrete uniqueness. In one of his letters to Frances, the woman he was to marry, the young G. K. Chesterton, reflecting the trinitarian view, already had a profound grasp of this: "I do not think there is anyone who takes quite such a fierce pleasure in things being themselves as I do. The startling wetness of water excites and intoxicates me; the fieriness of fire, the steeliness of steel, the unutterable muddiness of mud. It is just the same with people. . . . When we call a man 'manly' or a woman 'womanly' we touch the deepest philosophy."[9]

There is a phrase in the Apostles' Creed that underscores both the personal and the material dimensions of particularity or otherness expressive of that "deepest philosophy" rooted in the Trinity: "the resurrection of the body." These words affirm that although our being will be gloriously transformed through resurrection, our eternal form of existence will be in continuity with the unique body-soul-spirit person we are now. We will never lose our unique personal identity and be submerged into one.

Likewise, in the Christian understanding of the church, the strong emphasis on *koinonia* and unity is never at the expense of personal particularity and otherness (1 Corinthians 12:7-27; Ephesians 4:1-16). As Catherine Mowry LaCugna maintains,

> The communion of persons in the Spirit does not entail a leveling to the lowest common denominator. *Koinonia* does not swallow up the individual nor obscure his or her uniqueness and unique contribution, nor take away individual freedom by assimilating it into a collective will. The goal of Christian community, constituted by the Spirit in union with Jesus Christ, is to provide a place in which *everyone* is accepted as an ineffable, unique, and unrepeatable image of God, irrespective of how the dignity of a person might otherwise be determined: level of intelligence, political correctness, physical beauty, monetary value.[10]

In John's heavenly vision, the innumerable multitude that stands and worships before the throne of God is "from every nation, from all tribes and peoples and languages" (Revelation 7:9). Heaven is not a homogenous place but one where the particularities of nations, tribes, peoples and languages remain.

Lamin Sanneh, a native of Gambia, West Africa, is professor of missions and world Christianity at Yale Divinity School. In an age when it is fashionable to condemn the cultural imperialism and religious bigotry of Christian missions during the colonial period (1820-1960), he insists that despite all their shortcomings, the missionaries of that era certainly did one thing right: they translated the Scriptures into the vernacular of peoples. Consequently, they paved the way for the remarkable growth of Christianity in the postcolonial period: "Bible translation into the mother tongue has opened the way for the worldwide Christian renewal and for the diverse cultural expressions that have become the vintage mark of the religion as a global phenomenon."[11]

Sanneh, who grew up in a devout Muslim family in Gambia, notes the stark contrast at this point between Christianity and Islam, which frowns on translating the Qur'an and insists that only the original Arabic version can be used for prescribed acts of worship and devotion. To be sure, Muslims may use translations of the Qur'an for private study, but "not for the stipulated acts of public worship and certainly not as a substitute for the original."[12]

In translating the Bible into the vernacular, Christian missionaries shouldered a heavy burden as they grappled with issues such as alphabet, script, text, tone, orthography, semantics, grammar, usage, culture and dynamic equivalence. What caused them to do it? Was it just a tactic to win converts, as critics often contend? The real reason, Sanneh maintains, was "an acknowledgment that languages have intrinsic merit for communicating the divine message. They are worthy of God's attention."[13]

Sanneh doesn't probe deeper to consider why the Christian God regards languages as worthy of attention, but the answer lies in God's nature as Trinity. God's esteem for the particularity of human languages ultimately flows out of his esteem for the otherness and particularity in himself. In the absolute monotheism of Islam, Allah speaks in one language; in the triune theism of Christianity, the Father, Son and Holy Spirit speak in many.

There are other implications of this characteristic of trinitarian life for a Christian worldview. For example, it leads to the belief that each person matters immensely. Like a shepherd who leaves the ninety-nine sheep to find the one that is lost (Luke 15:3-7), so God cares about each man, each woman, each child. As Michael Ramsey states,

"The infinite worth of the one is the key to the Christian understanding of the many."[14]

There is also a wide range of implications for the practice of ministry. Consider, for example, how in evangelism and mission it leads to an incarnational approach that takes into account the personal and cultural uniqueness of those we are attempting to reach. Furthermore, think about how in congregational life it underscores the importance of helping individual members discover their particular ministries based on their heart passions, spiritual gifts, natural talents, personality and life experiences. Finally, see how it calls every congregation to affirm and reflect in a variety of ways the multicultural, multiracial diversity of the body of Christ.

LEARNING TO ACCEPT OURSELVES

In drawing out the implications of otherness and particularity for the vocation of ministry, however, I want to focus on an issue that scores of persons in ministry struggle with: self-acceptance. Although we may have a difficult time with the otherness and particularity of other persons (especially others in the body of Christ), we often have an even more difficult time with the otherness and particularity of *ourselves*. Years ago Carl Jung expressed the problem well:

> The acceptance of oneself is the essence of the whole moral problem and the epitome of a whole outlook on life. That I feed the hungry, that I forgive an insult, that I love my enemy in the name of Christ—all these are undoubtedly great virtues. What I do unto the least of my brethren, that I do unto Christ. But what if I should discover that the least amongst them all, the poorest of all the beggars, the most impudent of all the offenders, the very enemy himself—that these are within me, and that

I myself **stand** in need of the alms of my own kindness—that I myself am the enemy who must be loved—what then? As a rule, the Christian's attitude is then reversed; there is no longer any question of love or long-suffering; we say to the brother within us "Raca," and condemn and rage against ourselves.[15]

Over the years as I have counseled with people in ministry and wrestled with myself, I have come to believe Jung is right. We often find it much easier to extend grace to others than to ourselves. We accept their faults and failures but incessantly nag at ourselves. Our inner voice is relentless and demanding: *You should have . . . you could have . . . you ought to have done or not done that!*

In recent years, numerous Christian authors have rightly urged us to pay attention to this matter of self-acceptance. For example, Brennan Manning claims that in almost thirty years as a "vagabond evangelist," self-hatred is the predominant spiritual problem he has encountered.[16] Henri Nouwen maintains that more than popularity, success or pride, "self-rejection is the greatest enemy of the spiritual life because it contradicts the sacred voice that calls us the 'Beloved.'"[17] My father, David Seamands, calls low self-esteem "Satan's deadliest weapon" because it paralyzes our potential, destroys our dreams, ruins our relationships and sabotages our service.[18]

Leanne Payne considers our inability to accept ourselves one of the three main barriers to spiritual and emotional wholeness in Christ. She believes that self-acceptance is a Christian virtue and quotes Romano Guardini, the Catholic philosopher-theologian: "The act of self-acceptance is the root of all things. I must agree to be the person who I am. Agree to have the qualifications which I have. Agree to live within the limitations set for me. . . . The clarity and the courageousness of this acceptance is the foundation of all existence."[19]

Of course, there is a fallen, sinful self that Scripture says must be denied (Mark 8:34) and put to death (Romans 6:6; Ephesians 4:22-3). Earlier we saw how that "old self" stands in direct opposition to sacrificial, self-giving love.

But there is a new self, our authentic self, that is loved by God and is therefore to be accepted and nourished (Ephesians 4:24). In fact, only as we accept our authentic self are we free to love others. As Payne maintains, "If we are busy hating that soul that God loves and is in the process of straightening out, we cannot help others—our minds will be riveted on ourselves—not on Christ who is our wholeness."[20]

Thus gracious self-acceptance, delighting in ourselves because God loves and delights in us, is an essential aspect of spiritual and emotional maturity. And for those of us in ministry, the process of moving toward self-acceptance is often closely bound up with our ministry itself. In considering what it involves, I want to focus on three crucial elements in the process, using my own journey toward self-acceptance as an example.

1. *Renouncing the false self.* Originally Adam and Eve were "naked and were not ashamed" (Genesis 2:25), but as a result of their sinful disobedience they were afraid because they were naked (Genesis 3:10). So they covered themselves with fig leaves to hide from one another and crouched behind a tree to hide from God. We do that too. Fearful of rejection and abandonment, like Adam and Eve we hide our naked, fragile selves from God, from one another and even from ourselves.

And we do it by constructing a false self to hide from our true self. As Simon Tugwell describes it,

Like runaway slaves, we either flee our own reality or manufacture a false self which is mostly admirable, mildly prepossess-

ing, and superficially happy. We hide what we know or feel
ourselves to be (which we assume to be unacceptable and un-
lovable) behind some kind of appearance which we hope will
be more pleasing. We hide behind pretty faces which we put on
for the benefit of our public. And in time we may even come to
forget that we are hiding, and think that our assumed pretty
face is what we really look like.[21]

God calls us, like he called Adam, to come out of hiding. He loves
us—naked, vulnerable and fragile as we are. Fig leaves and makeup
don't make us more presentable to God. To answer the call, however,
we must turn away from the false self.

What does your false self look like? Let me tell you about mine.
He is a perfectionist who insists I measure up to his standards. His
three major "fig leaves" are accomplishment, acceptance and acclaim.

Because I believed his lies, from the time I was a teenager, I com-
pensated for my deep-seated fear of being exposed as inadequate by
overachieving. When I was a senior in high school, I was voted "Most
Likely to Succeed," and in the years that followed I did everything in
my power to ensure that I did. As a student, a pastor and a professor,
I set high performance standards for myself. My identity and sense of
well-being were bound up with accomplishing them. When I fell
short, I would get angry with myself and sometimes depressed.

My perfectionist false self says I have to be loved and accepted by
everyone. According to his standard, no one can criticize or disap-
prove of me. Everyone has to like me and hold me in high esteem.
Not only do I have to make myself worthwhile by performing well,
but other people have to be impressed with my performance. I have
to be admired and famous and must receive acclaim and applause for
my accomplishments.

A number of years ago, I had a visual image that revealed the nature of my false self. I saw myself as a juggler in a crowded circus tent, a picture of intense concentration. Sweat poured off my forehead as I worked to keep all the pins I was juggling in the air. The crowd sitting in the bleachers seemed indifferent toward me, and I was afraid that if any of the pins fell to the ground, they would stand up and walk out.

God's message to me through that picture was also clear: "Steve, that's you—always working hard, trying to prove to yourself and to others that you're competent, afraid of being rejected and desperately needing others' approval and applause to be convinced of your worth."

Accomplishment, acceptance and acclaim have been the fig leaves of my false self. Removing them has been an important part of my journey toward self-acceptance. And it's been amazing how God has used each of my various ministry settings to expose and then strip them away. In one of my pastorates, for example, I found myself caught in a crossfire of criticism as I began to lead the church in new directions. It was then that my acceptance fig leaf was exposed for what it was. For the first time, I saw with devastating clarity what an idol I had made of others' acceptance and approval and how desperately I needed to be liked by everyone. I wasn't an alcoholic, but I certainly was an "approvalholic."

One day during that time of pruning as I drove alone in my car, the Lord asked me a penetrating question: "Steve, isn't my love and approval of you enough? Do you have to have everyone else's too?" *Ouch!*

In that moment I saw myself as Adam in the Garden, and I realized what I had been doing. God was saying, "Eat the fruit of all the trees. You have my unconditional blessing and approval." But my false self countered, "That's not enough. I've got to have the forbidden fruit. I've got to have everyone else's approval too."

I realized the utter sinfulness of what I was doing and cried out, "Lord, forgive me. Cleanse my heart and set me free. Tear off this approval fig leaf I've worn so long."

In the months that followed, God answered my prayer. He brought me to the place where his approval was enough and I didn't have to have everyone else's. Now I can even give people permission not to like me!

What are the fig leaves of your false self? Are you willing to let God expose and strip them away? For those of us in vocational ministry, one of the fig leaves we are often tempted to hide behind is our ministerial persona—the omnicompetent, affable ministerial self we present to those around us. Some of us have worn that fig leaf so long we're afraid that if it's stripped away, there will be nothing underneath it.

In order to accept our true self, the false self must first be revealed so it can be renounced and put to death. Before you can "clothe [yourself] with the new self," you first must "put away . . . your old self" (Ephesians 4:22-24).

2. *Removing the seeds of self-rejection.* The seeds of self-rejection from which the false self emerges are generally planted in our formative childhood years. As a result of our dysfunctional family life, a lack of unconditional love and experiences of personal trauma, a false self takes root and develops to alleviate our pain and meet our needs for love, intimacy, affirmation and acceptance. Brennan Manning describes how during a twenty-day personal retreat he finally came to terms with what had happened in his childhood:

> As the days passed, I realized that I had not been able to *feel* anything since I was eight years old. A traumatic experience at that time shut down my memory for the next nine years and my feelings for the next five decades.

When I was eight, the impostor, or false self, was born as a defense against pain. The impostor within whispered, "Brennan, don't ever be your real self anymore because nobody likes you as you are. Invent a new self that everyone will admire and nobody will know." So I became a good boy—polite, well-mannered, unobtrusive, and deferential. I studied hard, scored excellent grades, won a scholarship in high school, and was stalked every waking moment by the terror of abandonment and the sense that nobody was there for me.

I learned that perfect performance brought the recognition and approval I desperately sought. I orbited into an unfeeling zone to keep fear and shame at a safe distance.[22]

Unlike Manning's, the seeds of my false self weren't planted through a traumatic childhood experience but by growing up in the shadow of a very successful father. During his ministry he was a distinguished missionary, outstanding preacher, gifted counselor and bestselling author. As a result, I grew up believing a lie that if I was to be somebody, I had to measure up to the standard Dad had set. I had to be successful in ministry like he was. Furthermore, other people had to notice me and my accomplishments the way they noticed his.

It was during my early years as a professor at Asbury Theological Seminary that I came to realize how profoundly that lie had affected me. We have some tremendously gifted persons on our faculty. When I first began working among them, I often found myself discouraged, feeling like a little frog in a big pond, like a sapling in the shadow of towering trees.

Soon I was struggling with feelings of jealousy toward certain faculty colleagues and found myself competing with them. In my mind, I had to be a more popular professor, a more productive writer and a more sought-after speaker than they were. When I perceived that they were accomplishing more than I was, it made me depressed.

Then God began to reveal to me how growing up in the shadow of my father had affected me. I had believed a lie that in and of myself I wasn't worthwhile; to be worthwhile I had to be as productive, popular and prominent as he was. In the soil of that lie the seeds of my false self were planted.

Of course, that lie was absolutely antithetical to what I believed and taught about God's unconditional love and acceptance. Our self-worth is not based on what we do or what others think of us. It has nothing to do with how large our congregation is, how well we preach, lead or counsel, how many books we write or how famous we are. It is simply a gift from God. In Christ we are declared to be God's beloved children (Romans 1:7; 1 John 3:1). I realized that in seeking to establish my self-worth on the basis of accomplishments, acceptance and acclaim, I was spurning God's free gift.

As I became increasingly aware of what I was doing and why I was doing it, I desperately wanted to stop but still found myself falling into familiar performance-oriented patterns. Finally I admitted that I was in bondage to the false self and began to cry out to God to heal me and set me free.

In a chapel service at the seminary the Lord answered my prayer. It wasn't dramatic or emotional, but during the preaching of the sermon, as the psalmist expressed it, "he sent out his word and healed [me]" (Psalm 107:20). At some deep level, the brokenness within me was mended. I was set free from my bondage to the false self, set free not to have to follow in my father's footsteps, set free to be the unique person God has created me to be.

Your journey to self-acceptance will no doubt be quite different from Brennan Manning's and from mine. But like ours, yours will involve turning over the soil in which the seeds of self-rejection were planted and uprooting the lies of the false self.

3. *Receiving our acceptance from Christ.* Self-acceptance is not something we talk ourselves into; neither is it a form of narcissism. The Christian perspective differs profoundly from what is advocated in much popular therapeutic self-help literature. As C. S. Lewis says, "Your real, new self . . . will not come as long as you are looking for it. It will come when you are looking for Him."[23] Just as the persons of the Trinity find their unique identities by focusing not on themselves but on one another, so Christian self-acceptance comes as we look to God and hear him say, "My child, you are accepted in the Beloved."

Chapter three stressed that knowing we are beloved, experiencing the divine embrace, is the foundation of Christian ministry. Now I am saying that it is the foundation of true self-acceptance as well. For having heard him say, "You are accepted," we are then truly able to accept ourselves. Self-acceptance is thus a gift, a work of grace wrought in our heart through the Holy Spirit. Our part is to receive the gift, to accept ourselves on the basis of God's acceptance.

An important step in my journey toward self-acceptance came when I realized that by insisting on establishing my self-worth on the basis of accomplishments, acceptance and acclaim, I was rejecting God's gift. Worse than that, I was playing God. For by living according to the standards of the false self, I was defining what made me acceptable instead of accepting God's definition. To reject God's way and insist on our own is sin. Acknowledging it as such and repenting of it was a crucial step in my journey, and one that I must repeat whenever the false self raises its ugly head and tempts me to live according to its definition rather than God's.

4. *Embracing our weaknesses.* As a result of his "thorn in the flesh"

which God chose not to remove, Paul learned that God's power is made perfect in weakness. So he declared, "I will boast all the more gladly of my weaknesses, so that the power of Christ may dwell in me" (2 Corinthians 12:9). Learning to embrace our weaknesses and limitations as Paul did is an important part of self-acceptance. In fact, since our false self generally can't tolerate weakness, this is an important way to renounce it and put it to death.

Barbara was disappointed when I gave her a B+ on a class paper, so she came by my office to talk about it. I knew that in addition to her seminary classes she was working a demanding job and seeing a counselor about some unresolved emotional issues, so I praised her for doing as well on the paper as she had. Then I suggested that given all she was involved in that semester, she should accept her academic limitations and give herself permission to get B's instead of A's.

"No way," she retorted. "I've always been an A student, and I won't settle for anything less."

We discussed the issue for a while. I tried to convince her that it is a mark of maturity, a sign of strength, not weakness, to accept our limitations, but she wouldn't hear of it. Getting impatient, I finally asked, "Barbara, have you asked Jesus what he thinks about your B+? Do you think he'll be upset with you if you don't get straight A's this semester."

She blushed and then hesitatingly replied, "I'm afraid to ask him."

"Afraid?" I said, somewhat puzzled. "What are you afraid of?"

I'll never forget her answer: "I'm afraid that his standards will be lower than mine."

She was right. Christ's standards were "lower" than those of her perfectionist false self. Of course he wanted Barbara to do her best, but this semester, given all that she had to juggle, that was a B+, not an A.

Our true selves—the selves Jesus loves and accepts and gave his life for—are both strong and weak, gifted and broken. We must learn to accept ourselves as he accepts us, especially the weak and broken parts that our false self rejects.

One day a woman was traveling on an interstate highway, sitting in the back seat of a car, looking out the window. Because the sun was shining brightly, all the window's flaws and imperfections stood out. As the woman noticed one particular scratch and focused on it, the perfectionist in her thought, *This window is no good. It ought to be replaced.*

But then she noticed something else. As the sunlight was refracted through the scratch, it was transformed into a tiny but exquisite rainbow. *I can focus on the flawed window,* she thought, *or I can focus on the beauty of the rainbow.* She chose the rainbow.

In like fashion, self-acceptance involves learning to embrace our flaws. Like Paul, we learn to glory in our weaknesses, for through them God's power is made perfect. God accepts and uses them; we must learn to accept them too.

John Eagan, an unheralded high school teacher in Milwaukee, Wisconsin, spent thirty years faithfully ministering to youth. He kept a journal, which was published shortly after his death in 1987. The introduction reads, "The point of John's journal is that we ourselves are the greatest obstacle to our own nobility of soul—which is what sanctity means. We too judge ourselves unworthy servants, and that judgment becomes a self-fulfilling prophecy. We deem ourselves too inconsiderable to be used even by a God capable of miracles with no more than mud and spit. And thus our false humility shackles an otherwise omnipotent God."[24]

Eagan was a flawed, broken man with weaknesses and character defects, but he had learned through Christ to accept himself. His breakthrough came during a retreat when he was visiting with Bob, his spiritual director. With great clarity Bob said, "John, the heart of it is this: to make the Lord and his immense love for you constitutive

of your personal worth. *Define yourself radically as one beloved by God.*
God's love for you and his choice of you constitute your worth. Accept that, and let it become the most important thing in your life."[25]

GRACE FOR OURSELVES

The eternal particularity and otherness of the three persons whom we call Father, Son and Holy Spirit remind us that God cherishes and delights in the uniqueness of each human being. Have you learned to cherish and delight in yourself and all that you are as God cherishes and delights in you? Have you celebrated the fact that you have a story and calling unlike those of any other person? Have you come to the point of gracious self-acceptance?

George Bernanos's classic *A Diary of a Country Priest* contains the thoughts and reflections of a Roman Catholic priest who for years faithfully carried out his ministry in a small French village. Throughout his life and ministry he struggled with doubts and insecurities. However, the last entry in his diary reveals that he finally came to a place of personal peace and self-acceptance:

> It's all over now. The strange mistrust I had of myself, of my own being, has flown, I believe forever. That conflict is done. I am reconciled to myself, to the poor, poor shell of me. How easy it is to hate oneself! True grace is in forgetting; yet if pride could die in us, the supreme grace would be to love oneself in all simplicity as one would love any member of the Body of Christ. Does it really matter? Grace is everywhere.[26]

How significant it is in our life and ministry when we too arrive at the place where, knowing we have been loved and accepted by God, we can love and embrace ourselves, since grace is everywhere—even grace for ourselves.

SEVEN

MUTUAL INDWELLING

The Reciprocity of Trinitarian Ministry

The whole of our consciousness is meant to be interpenetrated
with the consciousness of His indwelling life and mind and will and love,
even as the air in summer is transfused with sunshine.

J. SIDLOW BAXTER

❖

In 1865, having served as a missionary in China for six years, Hudson Taylor founded the China Inland Mission while he was on furlough in England. Taylor's vision was to take the gospel beyond the coastal cities, where it had already been planted, into China's heartland. The policies and practices of the new mission were radical for the colonial period: it was interdenominational, no formal education was required of missionaries, unmarried women could serve, Chinese dress was worn, and final decision-making authority rested in China, not back in England.

The following year, thirty-four-year-old Taylor, his family and sixteen young missionaries who had joined the mission sailed to China to begin the work. The CIM, as it came to be called, grew until in

1895 it numbered 641 missionaries serving in all of China's provinces except for several border regions.

Today when the leaders of China's vibrant house-church movement share their vision of raising up 100,000 Chinese missionaries who will complete the task of the Great Commission by evangelizing people throughout Muslim, Hindu and Buddhist strongholds, they often point to the influence and inspiration of Hudson Taylor. As Peter Xu Yongze, a key figure in the Back to Jerusalem movement, explains,

> The vision of the house churches in China today is not only to saturate our own country with the life and presence of the Lord Jesus Christ, but also to impact all the remaining Muslim, Buddhist and Hindu nations with the gospel. This is why we are so thankful for the impact Hudson Taylor made on our country. His example was one of single minded passion to see God's kingdom come. Like a mighty soldier he marched into pioneer areas where the name of Jesus Christ had never been uttered before.
>
> Today the house churches in China have caught that same vision. It is as though Hudson Taylor handed a flaming torch to the Chinese church and asked us to continue the race towards the finish line.[1]

Why was God able to so significantly accomplish his purposes through Hudson Taylor that he is still having a major impact on the world today? In *Hudson Taylor's Spiritual Secret,* published in 1932, Howard and Geraldine Taylor, his son and daughter-in-law, reveal the key to his fruitful life and ministry.

Early in 1869, three years after he had returned to China, Taylor experienced a "dark night of the soul." The death of his eight-year-old daughter, intense political unrest and the responsibility he carried for the missionaries under his care weighed him down. In a letter

to his mother he poured out his heart concerning his growing awareness of his lack of spiritual power:

> My position becomes continually more and more responsible
> and my need greater of special grace to fill it. But I have contin-
> ually to mourn that I follow at such a distance and learn so
> slowly to imitate my precious Master.
>
> I cannot tell you how I am buffeted sometimes by tempta-
> tions. I never knew how bad a heart I have. . . . Often I am
> tempted to think that one so full of sin cannot be a child of God
> at all. . . . Pray that the Lord will keep me from sin, will sanctify
> me wholly, will use me more largely in His service.[2]

Six months later, Taylor's prayer was answered through a letter he
received from a fellow missionary, John Macarthy. Explaining what
he had recently discovered about the life of holiness, Macarthy
quoted from a book entitled *Christ Is All,* stressing that the problem
with many who earnestly pursue holiness is defective faith. Because
they have a faith that seeks but not a faith that rests, the joyful confidence of abiding in Christ eludes them. Macarthy then noted how
their faith could be transformed:

> How then to have our faith increased? Only by thinking of all
> that Jesus is and all He is for us: His life, His death, His work,
> He Himself as revealed to us in the Word, to be the subject of
> our constant thoughts. Not a striving to have faith . . . but a
> looking off to the Faithful One seems all we need; a resting in
> the Loved One entirely, for time and for eternity.[3]

When Hudson Taylor read those words on Saturday, September 4,
1869, in the little mission station at Chin-kiang, the scales fell off his
eyes and he perceived his union with Christ as never before. He re-

counted what happened in a letter to his sister:

> As I read, I saw it all! "If we believe not, he abideth faithful." I
> looked to Jesus and saw (and when I saw, oh, how joy flowed!)
> that He had said, "I will never leave thee."
>
> "Ah, *there* is rest!" I thought. "I have striven in vain to rest
> in Him. I'll strive no more. For has not *He* promised to abide
> with *me*—never to leave me, never to fail me? And, dearie, *He
> never will.*
>
> Nor was this all He showed me, nor one half. As I thought of
> the Vine and the branches, what light the blessed Spirit poured
> direct into my soul! How great seemed my mistake in wishing
> to get the sap, the fullness *out* of Him! I saw not only that Jesus
> will never leave me, but that I am a member of His body, of His
> flesh and of His bones. . . .
>
> I am dead and buried with Christ—ay, and risen too! And
> now Christ lives in me, and "the life that I now live in the flesh,
> I live by the faith of the Son of God, who loved me and gave
> himself for me."[4]

Taylor had been serving God as a missionary for nine years, but
from that day forward his life and ministry were on a different plane.
Galatians 2:20 had become an experiential reality. He had discovered
that restful sense of sufficiency in Another.

In Isaiah 40:31, the Hebrew verb *chalaph,* which is usually translated "renew"—"those who wait for the LORD shall *renew* their
strength"—conveys the idea of exchanging one thing for another.
Taylor knew that to be true. "The exchanged life," his favorite expression to describe it, was his "spiritual secret." His ministry became an
embodiment of the truth that the ministry we enter is the ministry *of*
Jesus Christ.

MUTUAL INDWELLING IN THE TRINITY

Yet the exchanged life Hudson Taylor came to know and experience is only a dim reflection of the characteristic of trinitarian life we want to consider now: mutual indwelling and interpenetration. The Father, Son and Holy Spirit, by virtue of their eternal love, live and dwell in each other to such an extent that they are one. In 1442 the Council of Florence expressed it like this: "The three persons are one God not three Gods. . . . Because of this unity the Father is entirely in the Son, entirely in the Holy Spirit, the Son is entirely in the Father, entirely in the Holy Spirit, the Holy Spirit is entirely in the Father, entirely in the Son."[5]

In affirming the mutual indwelling and interpenetration of the triune persons, the Council made explicit what is only implicit in Scripture. Jesus alludes to it when he says, "I am in the Father and the Father is in me" (John 14:11; cf. 10:38). He is speaking of the mutual indwelling of the Father and the incarnate Son, but his declaration also points to the mutual indwelling of the Father and the *pre*incarnate Son from all eternity.

Throughout Paul's writings, he also points to the coinherence of the persons of the Trinity. In Romans 8:9-11, for example, Paul interchanges the Father, Son and Holy Spirit in a way that implies their mutual indwelling and participation in one another:

> But you are not in the flesh; you are in the Spirit, since the Spirit of God dwells in you. Anyone who does not have the Spirit of Christ does not belong to him. But if Christ is in you, though the body is dead because of sin, the Spirit is life because of righteousness. If the Spirit of him who raised Jesus from the dead dwells in you, he who raised Christ from the dead will give life to your mortal bodies also through his Spirit that dwells in you.

Commenting on this passage, David Cunningham observes,

> Here, as often, Paul's language seems to refer to the Three *not* as
> individuals who happen to have come into relation with each
> other, but rather to a reality that is so mutually self-participative
> that distinctions can no longer be drawn. Thus he can claim
> that justification comes "in the name of the Lord Jesus Christ
> and in the Spirit of our God" (1 Cor. 6:11); that "No one can say
> 'Jesus is Lord' except by the Holy Spirit" (1 Cor. 12:3); and even
> that "the Lord is the Spirit" (2 Cor 3:17-18).[6]

As the doctrine of the Trinity developed in the church and theologians searched for language to describe the mutual indwelling and interpenetration of the three persons, they eventually landed on the beautiful Greek term *perichoresis*. Perichoresis conveys a number of ideas: reciprocity, interchange, giving to and receiving from one another, being drawn to one another and contained in the other, interpenetrating one another by drawing life from and pouring life into one another as a fellowship of love.

Yet while perichoresis involves permeation, there is no blurring of differences or merging with one another. There is coinherence but without commingling or coalescence. Distinctions between the trinitarian persons are thus maintained, along with their essential dynamic unity. As Jürgen Moltmann indicates, "The doctrine of perichoresis links together in a brilliant way the threeness and the unity, without reducing the threeness to the unity, or dissolving the unity in the threeness."[7]

The earliest theological use of this term was in discussions concerning the two natures of Christ. Theologians like Gregory Nazianzen and Maximus the Confessor used it to portray the mutual indwelling and interpenetration of the divine and human actions of the one person of Christ. Like a red-hot knife that performs the distinct actions of cutting and burning simultaneously, a perichoresis of divine and human actions is performed by the one person of Christ.

Perichoresis was first used in reference to the Trinity in the sixth century by a writer known to us as "pseudo-Cyril" and was popularized in the eighth century through the writings of John of Damascus. As John described the trinitarian persons,

> They are inseparable and cannot part from one another, but keep to their separate courses within one another, without coalescing or mingling, but cleaving to each other. For the Son is in the Father and the Spirit; and the Spirit in the Father and the Son; and the Father in the Son and the Spirit but there is no coalescence or commingling or confusion. And there is one in the same motion: For there is one impulse and one motion of the three subsistences, which is not to be observed in any created nature.[8]

Several different analogies have been used to picture the perichoresis of the Trinity. It is like three sources of light in the same room, interpenetrating each other so that the resulting light is single yet somehow remains multiple. Or like the three notes of a major triad, which when played together indwell each other and create the one sound of the chord even while retaining their distinct identities. Or like the three dimensions of physical objects, height, depth and width. Each dimension implies the other two, so that changing any one of the three changes the whole.

Western theologians used two Latin words, *circuminsessio* and *circumincessio*, to translate the Greek *perichoresis*. Together they bring out the passive and active senses of *perichoresis*. *Circuminsessio*, literally "seated in another," means that one person indwells the space of another and is contained in another. This translation, which was preferred by Thomas Aquinas, suggests a state of being, a completed act, and conveys the passive sense of *perichoresis. Circumincessio,* by contrast, is a more active word. The translation preferred by Bonaventure, it connotes a state of doing, of interpenetration, of moving in and through the other, and "refers to the entry of each divine person into the life of the others in total openness and freedom."[9]

In order to convey this more active sense of *perichoresis,* theologians in the Middle Ages used the image of a divine dance. The Greek noun *perichoresis,* they noted, is closely related to *perichoreuo,* the Greek verb that literally means "to dance around" or "to dance in a circle" (derived from the noun *choreia,* dance, from which we get our English word *choreography*). Scholars today generally agree that although the philological evidence doesn't indicate that *perichoresis* is directly derived from *perichoreuo,* their close association and the play on words nicely underscore the dynamic sense of *perichoresis.*

In the perichoretic dance of the Trinity, says Paul Fiddes, "the partners not only encircle each other and weave in and out between each other as in human dancing; in the divine dance, so intimate is the communion that they move in and through each other so that the pattern is all-inclusive."[10] Catherine Mowry LaCugna elaborates further. The triune persons, she suggests, "experience one fluid motion of encircling, encompassing, permeating, enveloping, outstretching. There are neither leaders nor followers in the divine dance, only an eternal movement of reciprocal giving and receiving, giving again and receiving again. . . . The divine dance is fully personal and interpersonal, expressing the essence and unity of God."[11]

As *circuminsessio* and *circumincessio,* perichoresis is both passive and active, both rest and motion, both indwelling and interpenetration. In a sublime way, Rublev's icon portrays the *perichoresis* of the

Trinity. According to Orthodox theologians Leonide Ouspensky and Vladimir Lossky:

> [The icon has] action, expressed in gestures, communion expressed in the inclining of the heads and postures of the figures, and a silent motionless peace. This inner life, uniting the three figures enclosed in the circle and communicating itself to its surroundings, reveals the whole inexhaustible depth of this image. It echoes, as it were, the words of Saint Dionysius the Areopagite, according to whose interpretation "circular movement signifies that God remains identical with Himself, that He envelops in synthesis the intermediate parts and the extremities, which are at the same time containers and contained, and that He recalls to Himself all that has gone forth from Him."[12]

CHRIST IN YOU, THE HOPE OF GLORY

The trinitarian circle where the Father, Son and Holy Spirit indwell and are indwelt by one another is open, not closed. We have been invited into the circle to participate in the divine dance. In the incarnation of the Son, when the Word became flesh and dwelt among us (John 1:14), God's desire and intention to pour himself into us and draw us into himself is fully revealed. Through this act of self-giving, divinity flowed into humanity and humanity was drawn into divinity. In the person of Christ there was a copresence and coinherence of the divine and human natures, yet, as the Chalcedonian definition states, the two natures dwelt together "without confusion, without change, without division, without separation." Thus in the incarnation there is a profound mutual indwelling of God and humanity.

Of course, the way God indwells human beings is qualitatively different from the way we indwell God. Miroslav Volf expresses the difference like this: "The Spirit indwells human persons, whereas human beings by contrast indwell *the life-giving ambience of the Spirit,* not the person of the Spirit."[13] Only God, he maintains, can truly indwell other persons.

We must always keep this difference in mind, but we must also emphasize the reality of Christ's dwelling in us and our dwelling in him. To his disciples, Jesus declared not only "I am in the Father and the Father is in me" (John 14:11) but also "I am in my Father, and you in me, and I in you" (John 14:20). Later he prayed, "As you, Father, are in me and I am in you, may they also be in us" (John 17:21). What, then, is the importance of mutual indwelling for the Christian life and the vocation of ministry?

Hudson Taylor of England called it "the exchanged life"; Watchman Nee of China, "the normal Christian life"; Andrew Murray of South Africa, "the abiding life"; and Ruth Paxson of America, "life on the highest plane." Yet they all are describing the same spiritual reality: Christ's life indwelling the believer through the power of the Holy Spirit. Paxson expresses it well:

> To be a Christian is nothing less than to have the glorified Christ living in us in actual presence, possession and power. It is to have Him as *the Life of our life* in such a way and to such a degree that we can say even as Paul said, "To me to live is Christ." To be a Christian is to *grow up into Christ in all things:* it is to have that divine seed which was planted in our innermost spirit blossom out into a growing conformity to His perfect life. To be a Christian is to have Christ the life of our minds, our hearts, our will, so that it is Christ thinking through us, living through us, willing through us. It is increasingly to have no life but the life of Christ within us filling us with ever increasing measure.[14]

It is no accident that Paxson quotes Paul (Philippians 1:21), for no New Testament writer emphasizes the mutual indwelling of the Christ in the believer and the believer in Christ as he does. In fact, there is a growing consensus among New Testament scholars that *this* doctrine—what Albert Schweitzer labeled as Paul's "in Christ mysticism"—not justification by faith, forms the heart of Paul's theology and experience.[15] According to Adolf Deissmann, for Paul our indwelling relationship with Christ is like the air we breathe: "Just as the air of life, which we breathe, is 'in' us and fills us, and yet we at the same time live in this air and breathe it, so it is also with the Christ-intimacy of the Apostle Paul: Christ in him, he in Christ."[16]

Numerous passages in Paul's writings (Romans 6:3-11; 8:10; 2 Corinthians 13:5; Philippians 2:5; 3:8-10; Colossians 1:27; 3:1-4) convey his "in Christ" theology and experience, but Galatians 2:19-20 captures it best: "I have been crucified with Christ; and it is no longer I who live, but it is Christ who lives in me. And the life I now live in the flesh I live by faith in the Son of God [or 'by the faith of the Son of God'], who loved me and gave himself for me." Here, as Richard Hays observes, Paul "provocatively [denies] his own role as the acting 'subject' of his own life and [claims] that he has been supplanted in this capacity by Christ."[17]

Of course, Paul is not saying he has lost his personal identity. Though Christ lives in Paul, there is still a life that Paul lives. He is still Paul, and more truly Paul when Christ lives in him. As in the case of the perichoresis in the Trinity, Galatians 2:20 involves a coinherence of Christ and the believer without coalescence or commingling.

Sadu Sundar Singh of India often used the example of the iron a blacksmith places in a red-hot coal fire. Soon the iron turns red and begins to glow like the coals, so you can truly say that the iron is in the fire and the fire is in the iron. Yet we know that the iron is not the fire and the fire is not the iron. When the iron is glowing, the black-smith can bend it into any shape he desires, but it still remains iron. Likewise, he emphasized, "we still retain our personality when we allow ourselves to be penetrated by Christ."[18]

Such is the nature of the indwelling of Christ in the believer and the believer in Christ. And given that it is the ministry *of* Jesus Christ we have entered, what could be more important for the vocation of ministry? Only through the reality of the exchanged life can we fulfill our calling. Thankfully, as Paul emphasizes, "the one who calls you is faithful, and he will do this" (1 Thessalonians 5:24). The Lord Jesus, who calls us to live a holy and righteous life, to minister to human need, to go into all the world and preach the gospel, is the One who will do all these things in us and through us.

Like Taylor, however, most of us don't realize this until we have been involved in ministry for several years. We generally have to come to the end of ourselves and our own self-effort in ministry. After we have exhausted ourselves in our sincere attempts to minister *for* Christ, we are finally ready to acknowledge the truth of Christ's words "Apart from me you can do nothing" and to hear his invitation "Abide in me as I abide in you" (John 15:4-5). Only then do we come to know the reality of Christ who is our life and of our life as hid with Christ in God (Colossians 3:3-4).

Stephen Olford, who for many years served faithfully and effectively as pastor of Calvary Baptist Church in New York City, tells how he came to realize this:

> The greatest moment in my life was when I discovered that God expects nothing more or less of Stephen Olford than abject failure! And, even more importantly, only one Person can live the Christian life, and that is Christ Himself; and only as I

trust Him to live His life in me, can I possibly live the quality
of life that satisfies the heart of God and challenges the world
in which I witness.[19]

Have you come to that moment in your own life and ministry? Have
you heard Christ say, "All this time you've been sincerely trying to do
for me what I deeply desire to do *through* you"?

No doubt through our sincere religious self-determination we can
make things happen in ministry; we can be productive. But there is
a world of difference, as noted earlier, between being productive and
being fruitful. Only as we lay down our exhausting attempts to accomplish ministry in our own strength, only as we learn to "let it happen" by restfully abiding in him as he abides in us, will we "bear
much fruit . . . fruit that will last" (John 15:5, 16). The exchanged
life where Christ dwells in us even as we dwell in him is the key to
participating in the ongoing ministry of Jesus. It was Hudson Taylor's
spiritual secret; it is ours too.

DWELLING IN ONE ANOTHER

The mutual indwelling and interpenetration of the persons of the
Trinity not only leads to an exchanged life and ministry as Christ
abides in us and we abide in him; it also leads to an exchanged life
with others. As Cunningham suggests, what we see in the Trinity "can
help us begin to think about what it might mean to dwell in, and be
indwelt by, the lives of others."[20]

As human beings created in God's image, we have been endowed
with a general capacity to open ourselves to others. Without it, human relationships would not exist. Our most joyful and fulfilling experiences of intimacy in marriage, family and friendships are bound
up in knowing others and being known by them.

As Christians, because of the oneness we have with the Father, Son and Holy Spirit, we also experience spiritual unity with other believers beyond our general human capacity for oneness. Notice how Jesus' prayer for our unity as believers is predicated on our unity in the Father and the Son: "As you, Father, are in me and I am in you, may they also *be one in us*" (John 17:21 alternate translation). Likewise, the apostle John grounds our fellowship with one another in the fellowship we have "with the Father and with his Son Jesus Christ" (1 John 1:3; cf. 1:7).

Koinonia, the Greek word for fellowship that John and other New Testament writers often use (cf. Acts 2:42; 2 Corinthians 13:14; Philippians 1:5; 2:1), implies an intensely close relationship with one another beyond mere human camaraderie. The depth of togetherness it involves is foreign to granular Western individualism. The fellowship of Christ's body is thus not a cluster of individual saints but, as theologian Paul Stevens maintains, a *perichoretic* fellowship analogous to and participating in the Trinity, where the members "coinhere, interanimate, and pour life into one another without coalescence or merger."[21]

What are some aspects of ministry where we might experience such *koinonia* and mutual indwelling in one another? Let's consider four that are common to most persons in ministry: empathic listening, intercessory prayer, team ministry and marriage intimacy.

1. *Empathic listening.* In *Life Together,* his classic on Christian community, Dietrich Bonhoeffer maintains that

> the first service that one owes to others in the fellowship consists in listening to them. . . . It is God's love for us that He not only gives us His Word, but also lends us His ear. So it is His work that we do for our brother when we learn to listen to him.

Christians, especially ministers . . . forget that listening can be
a greater service than speaking.

. . . The ministry of listening has been committed to them by
Him Who is Himself the great listener, and Whose work they
should share. We should listen with the ears of God that we
may speak the Word of God.[22]

God has not only spoken to us (Hebrews 1:2) but has also listened to
us through his Son. Often the most significant way we can communicate God's love and concern for someone is by empathically listening to him or her.

To listen empathically, we must first suspend our preoccupation
with ourselves by laying aside our concerns, agendas and assumptions. Then we must open ourselves to others by entering into their
experiences and their interpretations of them. Thus, as Michael
Nichols points out, "the act of listening requires a submersion of the
self and immersion in the other."[23] When we submerge our self, however, we don't dissolve it. In fact, we discover our true self when in
self-giving acts like empathic listening we exist for other persons.

Nevertheless, empathic listening requires us to be receptive, not
creative. By stepping out of ourselves and setting aside our frame of
reference for other persons, we take them into ourselves and allow
them to indwell us. And we in turn, by acknowledging and affirming
their frame of reference, are allowed to indwell them. This is why empathic listening is so essential to our growth and development as persons. For as Nichols suggests, "Without being listened to we are shut
up in the solitude of our own hearts." But when other persons truly
listen to us, we indwell them and they indwell us, offering us the val-
idation that is "absolutely essential for sustaining the self-affirmation
known as self-respect."[24] Often in ministry, more than our spoken

words of truth and wisdom, our listening ears joined with the listening ears of Christ are the greatest catalyst for transformation and growth in the lives of others.

2. *Intercessory prayer.* "In intercession," Paul Fiddes says, "we meet others in the perichoresis, the divine dance of Father, Son and Spirit. . . . We enter into the life of prayer already going on within the communion of God's being."[25] According to Scripture, the risen, ascended Christ is currently engaged in this work. Paul declares, "Christ Jesus, . . . who is at the right hand of God, . . . intercedes for us" (Romans 8:34), and the author of Hebrews says that Christ "always lives to make intercession" for us (Hebrews 7:25).

When we intercede for others, then, we are not so much called to pray *to* Jesus on their behalf as we are called to pray *with* Jesus for them. As we dwell in him and he dwells us in us, we become co-laborers, partners with Christ in his work of intercession. Knowing this frees us from taking the burden of intercession on ourselves.

Amy Carmichael spent over fifty years ministering to disadvantaged children in South India. Early in her ministry she had a deep concern for young girls who were given to Hindu priests to serve as temple prostitutes. As she began to work against that practice, there came a point when the opposition—both human and demonic—grew so intense that she wanted to give up carrying the burden. Then she came to understand whose burden it really was:

> At last a day came when the burden grew too heavy for me; and then it was as though the tamarind trees about the house were not tamarind, but olive, and under one of these trees our Lord Jesus knelt alone. And I knew that this was His burden, not mine. It was He who was asking me to share it with Him, not I who was asking Him to share it with me. After that there

was only one thing to do; who that saw Him kneeling there could turn away and forget? Who could have done anything but go into the garden and kneel down beside Him under the olive trees?[26]

Like Carmichael, we need to perceive our role in intercession. It is primarily Christ's work, not ours, yet as he dwells in us and we dwell in him, we join him in it.

But not only are we joined with Christ, we are also joined with the persons we are praying for. We open ourselves and allow them to indwell us. We identify with them even to the point of being willing to suffer and sacrifice on their behalf.

Consider, for example what Nehemiah did when he heard the news that the walls and gates of Jerusalem were in ruins. He "sat down and wept, and mourned for days, fasting and praying before the God of heaven" (Nehemiah 1:4). Although he was a righteous man, in his prayer he confessed the sins of his people as if they were his own: "I now pray before you day and night . . . confessing the sins of the people of Israel, which we have sinned against you. Both I and my family have sinned. We have offended you deeply" (Nehemiah 1:6-7).

Daniel's intercession was similar. He too pleaded with God on behalf of the people "by prayer and supplication with fasting and sackcloth and ashes" (Daniel 9:3). No one was more righteous than Daniel, yet he prayed, "We have sinned and done wrong, acted wickedly and rebelled" (Daniel 9:5). Both of these intercessors deeply identified themselves with the people. They didn't pray, "Lord forgive *them*," but "Lord forgive *us*."

In intercession, then, we radically open ourselves to others. As we indwell them and they indwell us, their concerns and needs become ours. Not only do we become one with Christ in praying for them, but also one with them in praying on their behalf to God.

3. *Team ministry.* In *Jesus Driven Ministry,* Sri Lankan church leader Ajith Fernando shows how, in contrast to the common one-pastor model, team ministry "was the standard model of ministry in the New Testament."[27] Jesus sent his disciples out two by two (Mark 6:7; Luke 10:1). In Acts, Peter and John ministered together in Jerusalem and Samaria (Acts 3-4; 8:14). Paul and Barnabas, the first missionaries, were sent out as a team (Acts 13:2). When this team broke up, both of them took others with them in forming new teams (Acts 15:39-40). Even when Paul went to Rome as a prisoner, Luke was with him (Acts 27:2).

Of course, team ministry can take various shapes and forms, depending on the situation and the task. But there is a growing consensus today that we need to recover the New Testament model. Even many churches where the one-pastor model is normative are moving toward partnership in leadership on the basis of spiritual gifts.

But what does healthy team ministry look like? As a leader seeking to establish strong teams in his church, George Cladis searched for a biblical and theological model to guide him. He found it in the perichoretic image of the Trinity, where "the three Persons in God [are] in constant movement in a circle that implies intimacy, equality, unity yet distinction, and love."[28] So in *Leading the Team-Based Church,* Cladis presents perichoresis as an image to move toward, a goal to strive for in creating and sustaining spiritually vibrant and effective team ministry.

In a perichoretic team, as a result of indwelling together in God and one another, there is a collaboration and synergy that enables the individual members to transcend their own limitations. The resulting whole is larger than the sum of its parts. In his *Invitation to Theology,*

Michael Jinkins compares it to a skilled jazz ensemble. As the performers play their music, it flows from them and among them, moving them as they respond to one another. Those who are listening to the music are moved to respond too. "The music has a life of its own, a life that draws the musicians together while not diminishing their discrete identities. The music draws the observers into a very real participation in and through the music."[29] Regardless of the shape of our particular ministry, all of us need to be involved in perichoretic teams like that.

4. *Marriage intimacy.* In the deep body-and-soul intimacy of marriage, we experience, as nowhere else, the mutual indwelling of human persons in each other. When Adam "knew" his wife, Eve (Genesis 4:1), their two bodies, souls and minds were melded into one. God created them for each other so that they would fit together as a unity in diversity and know the closest union possible between two human beings yet without the loss of uniqueness.

However, this union, reflecting the Trinity and "signifying unto us the mystical union which exists between Christ and his church," as the traditional wedding ritual declares, turns out to be more than we bargained for. In *The Mystery of Marriage,* Mike Mason says it well:

[Marriage] is disturbingly intense, disruptively involving, and that is exactly the way it was designed to be. It is supposed to be more, almost, than we can handle. It was meant to be a lifelong encounter that would be much more rigorous and demanding than anything human beings ever could have chosen, dreamed of, desired, or invented on their own. . . . For that is its very purpose: to get us out beyond our depth, out of the shallows of our own secure egocentricity and into the dangerous and unpredictable depths of a real interpersonal encounter.[30]

To be indwelled by our spouse like this often means having them too close for comfort! The more we are drawn to them, the more the truth about our broken, egocentric self is exposed. Each day they call us to painful, practical expressions of self-denial and self-sacrifice.

When a husband and wife stay committed to one another in the face of each other's brokenness and sin, their intimacy grows and deepens. It is the fruit of their repentance as they confront the truth about themselves and the forgiveness they extend to each other.

It has been said that the best gift a mother and father can give to their children is to love each other well. Likewise, one of the best gifts married ministers can give to those they minister to is to love their own spouse well. As we do, not only will they see us being conformed to the image of Christ, but in that mutual indwelling, that wedding of two becoming one, they will be offered a foretaste of something greater, an anticipation of a marriage in heaven yet to come. "Blessed are those who are invited to the marriage supper of the Lamb" (Revelation 19:9).

E I G H T

PASSIONATE MISSION

The Impulse of Trinitarian Ministry

Mission has its origin in the heart of God. God is a fountain of sending love.
This is the deepest source of mission.

DAVID BOSCH

❖

The quiet, sleepy, two-stoplight, "Mayberry RFD" town of Wilmore, Kentucky, is home to two academic institutions: Asbury College, founded in 1890, and Asbury Theological Seminary, founded in 1923. I reside in Wilmore, am a "double-dipper" (graduate of both institutions) and have taught at the seminary for over twenty years. Each day as I drive home from work, I pass a life-size metal statue of Francis Asbury, American Methodism's famous pioneer bishop, after whom both institutions are named.

The consummate circuit-riding preacher, Asbury traveled more than 270,000 miles on horseback across the American frontier proclaiming the gospel. The words inscribed on the plaque at the base of the statue by its sculptor, Everette Wyatt, describe him well: "On horseback he trekked the yet uncharted wilderness paths to unnamed places wherever men had ventured. Extolling God to any ear that was bent, winning minds and hearts to our Lord and Savior Jesus Christ."

Whether he was fording streams, traversing swamps, crossing swollen rivers, scrambling over jagged rocks and crevices or groping through forests, perpetual motion was the mark of Asbury's ministry. In a 1782 journal entry he states, "When we came to New Hope Creek we could not ford it; so I crossed on a log." The following entry continues undaunted: "I am willing to travel and preach as long as I live; and I hope I shall not live long after I am unable to travel."[1] No one knew frontier America—the highways and byways, the settlements of people from Massachusetts to Georgia, from the Atlantic Ocean to the Ohio River—as well as Asbury. He probably visited more American homes than any one person before the Civil War.

In his engaging biography of Asbury, Darius Salter speaks of his "always-on-the-move *modus operandi*"[2] and of his motto "Live or die, I must ride" as "a kind of monasticism on a horse."[3] It is fitting, then, that the statue of Francis Asbury in Wilmore has him on horseback headed out of town, not riding into it, so that the horse's rear end is pointing at the college and the seminary named after him! I think he would have wanted it that way.

One wonders, though, given the extremely harsh conditions on the frontier, how in the world Asbury was able to carry out his mission. What he accomplished was truly amazing. Yet as "Tex" Evans considered what Asbury did, he found himself wondering about something else.

Once in the 1970s, when Evans was serving on the staff of the United Methodist Church's Board of Discipleship, he was invited to preach at the anniversary celebration of a small rural church in Maryland—one that Asbury visited frequently during his lifetime. To get to the church, Asbury had to ford a nearby river that would often flood during the heavy spring rains.

Prior to the service, the pastor, along with several lifelong members of the church, took Evans down to the river to show him the place where Asbury crossed on horseback. While they were there, the church member described what it was like when the water rose during times of flooding.

"Can you imagine Francis Asbury crossing it when it was like that?" one of them asked Evans.

"No, I sure can't," he replied.

"Let me tell you how I think he did it," another member chimed in. And he went on to explain in great detail how he thought Asbury forded the swollen river, guided his horse across the raging current and finally came out safely on the other side.

Evans listened politely until the man had finished his lengthy explanation. "That certainly is interesting," he replied. "I appreciate you telling me how you think Francis Asbury did it. But there's something else I want to know. Even more than knowing *how* he did it, I want to know *why* he did it." The man smiled but didn't answer. He seemed puzzled at Evans's response.

As they were driving back to the church, however, Tex Evans hastily scribbled down the thoughts that were flooding his mind. Setting aside the message he had prepared, he gave a sermon at the anniversary service called "Why Francis Asbury Did It."

I'm not sure what he said that morning, and later on Tex Evans himself couldn't remember either! He told my faculty colleague George Hunter, who heard him tell this story on more than one occasion before Evans died, that the content of his message was a blur to him, and since he had lost his scribbled notes, he had no way of jogging his memory.

Of course Evans's sermon could have taken several different directions, for there was, no doubt, more than one reason Asbury did it. But the bottom line was this: Francis Asbury crossed that treacherous, swollen river in Maryland and traversed the American frontier from one end to the other because he was caught up in something much bigger than himself. He was caught up in an outward movement beginning in God himself, a divine sending, an eternal trinitarian going. Someone has quipped that "two-thirds of God is Go." It was the divine go that kept Francis Asbury going. Because the Father, Son and Holy Spirit are on a mission, so was he.

This inextricable connection between Trinity and mission—the last, but certainly not the least, of the seven characteristics of trinitarian life—is what we will explore now. And again, we shall see how vital and foundational it is for the vocation of ministry.

THE MISSION OF GOD

Only since the mid-twentieth century, as a result of the trinitarian renaissance described earlier, have theologians and missiologists begun to grasp the relationship between Trinity and mission. Before that time, mission was often viewed in relation to the doctrines of salvation and the church. Christians were supposed to "go" in order to save souls from eternal damnation or to expand the church.

Then, following the lead of theologian Karl Barth, at a conference of the International Missionary Council held in Willingen, Germany, in 1952, the idea of the *missio Dei* (mission of God) surfaced for the first time. As the council declared, "The missionary movement of which we are a part has its source in the Triune God Himself."[4] Mission, then, was first an attribute of God before it was an activity of individual Christians or the church. It is derived from God's triune nature, from the *sending* of God, and should be grounded primarily in the doctrine of God, not the doctrine of salvation or the church. According to Scripture, God the Father sends the Son (John 3:17; 5:36; 6:57; Galatians 4:6; 1 John 4:9), the Father and the Son send the Holy Spirit (John 14:26; 15:26; Acts 2:33), and the Father, Son and Holy Spirit send the church into the world (Matthew 28:19-20; John 17:18; 20:21; Acts 1:8; 13:2-3).

God is therefore in his very essence a missionary God. As theologian Paul Stevens emphasizes, "Mission is God's own going forth—truly an *ekstasis* of God. He is Sender, Sent and Sending."[5] The Father is the first missionary, who goes out of himself in creating the world and sending the Son for our salvation. The Son is the second missionary, who redeems humanity and all creation through his life, death, resurrection and exaltation. The Holy Spirit is the third missionary, who creates and empowers the church, the fourth missionary, to go into the world.

This means, as Jürgen Moltmann maintains, that "it is not the church that has a mission of salvation to fulfill in the world; it is the mission of the Son and the Spirit through the Father that includes the church, creating a church as it goes on its way."[6] To be sure, the church is an instrument of God's mission, but God's mission precedes, initiates, defines and sustains the church in mission. Consequently, there is not mission because there is church; there is church because there is mission already—the mission of the triune God.

Mission, then, is not essentially a human activity undertaken by the church and its leaders out of obligation to the Great Commission, gratitude for what God has done for us, and the desperate plight of the world. It is God's own mission in which we are invited to participate. The church is not as much a sending agency as it is a sent agency. We are sent because the triune God is Sender (Father), Sent (Son) and Sending (Holy Spirit).

Theologians such as Moltmann have also stressed that the revelation of God in Scripture as Sender, Sent and Sending in relation to the world is a reflection of something deeper, something eternal in God.[7] As God is revealed in history (the economic Trinity), God has always been in himself (the immanent Trinity). The sending (*missio*), the going outside of himself toward creation that is revealed in the life, death and resurrection of Jesus Christ, has its foundation in an eternal sending or *missio* within God.

Theologians in the fourth and fifth centuries intimated at this when they emphasized the "eternal generation" of the Son from the Father. From all eternity and hence without beginning, they insisted, the Father "begets" or sends out the Son from his very being. Likewise, the Father "breathes" or sends out the Holy Spirit. The triune God's missions in the world revealed in the sending of the Son and the sending of the Spirit are thus grounded in these two antecedent missions—the generation of the Son and the procession of the Holy Spirit—in God's eternal being. Because the Father eternally moves out to the Son and the Holy Spirit, God, as Father, Son and Holy Spirit, moves out to create, redeem and renew the world.

But why is there such an eternal movement in God? Rather than existing as a solitary, self-sufficient person, why does the Father eternally move out of himself in begetting the Son and breathing out the Holy Spirit? Christians who have reflected on this question generally propose a simple answer: because God *is* love (1 John 4:8). As C. S. Lewis explains,

> All sorts of people are fond of repeating the Christian statement that "God is love." But they seem not to notice that the words "God is love" have no real meaning unless God contains at least two Persons. Love is something that one person has for another

person. If God was a single person, then before the world was made, He was not love. [Christians] believe that the living, dynamic activity of love has been going on in God forever and has created everything else.[8]

Lewis also points out that whenever love exists, in addition to the two persons involved, the lover and the beloved, there is a third reality: the spirit of love that unites them. In human love relationships, the spirit of love is a concrete relational bond but not a "person" as such. However, the eternal, infinite spirit of love that unites the two divine persons, the Father and the Son, is "such a live concrete thing that this union itself is also a Person"—the Holy Spirit.[9] For Christians, then, to say "God *is* love" is to say "God in three persons, blessed Trinity." God's eternal self-differentiation as Father, Son and Holy Spirit is because God is love.

God *is* love also means that God is self-diffusive and self-communicative. He has what Jonathan Edwards called "a disposition to abundant self-communication."[10] For it is the nature of love to go out of itself, to be other-centered, not self-centered. Pseudo-Dionysius, the sixth-century spiritual theologian, said it well: "Love does not permit the lover to rest in himself. It draws him out of himself, so that he may be entirely in the beloved."[11] God's going out of himself in first creating and then redeeming and renewing the world issues out of the plenitude of the Father, Son and Holy Spirit's love for each other. Out of the dynamic fullness of self-communicating love *within* the circle of the Trinity flows God's love for the world *outside* the circle. In fact, as Moltmann maintains, the trinitarian circle "cannot be conceived as a closed circle—the symbol of perfection and self-sufficiency." Because the trinitarian persons are eternally open to one another, the Trinity is "open for its own sending . . . 'open' in order that it may 'make itself open,' . . . open to man, open to the world and open to time."[12]

Jesus said, "As the Father has sent me, so I send you" (John 20:21). Our being sent is thus patterned after this divine sending. Furthermore, it participates in it, for it flows out of our relationship with God in Christ through the Holy Spirit—a relationship that, as we've seen, allows us to enter into the trinitarian circle and be caught up in the motion of other-centered love between the Father, Son and Holy Spirit flowing out to the world. As missiologist David Bosch maintains, "To participate in mission is to participate in the movement of God's love toward people, since God is a fountain of sending love."[13] So Jesus prays for his disciples "that the love with which you have loved me *may be in them,* and I in them" (John 17:26).

Resonance is a technical term physicists use to describe when two vibrating energies move toward each other and the frequency of their vibrations matches. This meaning is also reflected in our vernacular use of the word: when persons "resonate" with each other, we often say they are "on the same wavelength" or "in tune with each other." In both physics and interpersonal relationships, there is enormous energy in resonance. For example, when the wind passing through Puget Sound created a double oscillation that matched the frequency of the Tacoma Narrows Bridge in Washington, the bridge collapsed. Similarly, when Clemson University officials in South Carolina investigated why their football stadium was crumbling, they discovered that "Louie, Louie," a song often played by the marching band, gave off frequencies that perfectly matched the frequency of the stadium.[14]

When we are resonating with the eternal love frequencies of the Father, Son and Holy Spirit, there is also an enormous release of energy, and we are thrust forth in mission. Whenever mission flows out of something else—our ego needs, our attempts to earn God's ap-

proval or the approval of others, or even our response to the desperate plight of humanity—it has lost its ultimate ground and cannot be
sustained. In *So Send I You,* lectures to those preparing for missionary
service, Oswald Chambers articulates it well: "The need can never be
the call for missionary enterprise. The need is the opportunity. The
call is the commission of Jesus Christ and relationship to His Person.
'All power is given unto *me . . . go ye therefore.*' Any work for God that
has less than a passion for Jesus Christ as its motive will end in crush-
ing heartbreak and discouragement."[15] God's mission flows out of
love; our mission, which is patterned after and participates in God's,
must too.

Consequently, mission is more caught than taught, more divinely
imparted than humanly initiated. As we participate in the divine
dance of love, we are captured by the divine mission. Again, Lewis
says it well:

> The whole dance, or drama, or pattern of this three-Personal life
> is to be played out in each one of us; or (putting it the other way
> round) each one of us has got to enter that pattern, take his place
> in the dance. Good things as well as bad, you know, are caught
> by a kind of infection. If you want to get warm you must stand
> near the fire; if you want to be wet you must get into the water.
> If you want joy, power, peace, eternal life, you must get close to,
> or even into, the thing that has them. If you are close to it, the
> spray will wet you: if you are not, you will remain dry.[16]

THE ACTS OF THE HOLY SPIRIT

How then do we catch the divine infection? How do we get warmed
by the fire or wet in the water? The risen Christ tells us in his final
words to his disciples. In John's account, immediately after he said to

them, "As the Father has sent me, so I send you," he breathed on them and said, "Receive the Holy Spirit" (John 20:21-22). And in Luke's account, he stresses that "you will receive power when the Holy Spirit has come upon you; and you will be my witnesses in Jerusalem, in all Judea and Samaria, and to the ends of the earth" (Acts 1:8). The Holy Spirit, who is closely associated in Scripture with both fire (Luke 3:16-17; Acts 2:3) and water (John 7:37-39), connects us to the mission of the triune God. Through his presence in us we catch the divine infection, we participate in the Father, Son and Holy Spirit's love for one another and mission of love to the world.

The book of Acts reveals what that looked like in the lives of the apostles. Yet more than the story of the acts of the apostles, it is the story of the acts of the Holy Spirit empowering them in mission. Actually, it is the Holy Spirit's mission more than theirs. On the Day of Pentecost his mission is launched (Acts 2:1-4), and throughout Acts it remains central. The Holy Spirit is the One in charge, not the apostles. They are not leading but following the leader!

It is the Holy Spirit who arranges a chance meeting between Philip and an Ethiopian finance minister (Acts 8:26-40), prepares Ananias to accept arch-persecutor Saul as a brother (Acts 9:10-19) and persuades Peter to visit the house of Cornelius, a Gentile military officer (Acts 10:1-48). It is the Spirit who initiates the first mission to the pagan world (Acts 13:1-2), has the final say in the dispute at the Jerusalem Council (Acts 15:22-29), guides Paul to unexpected places on his missionary journeys (Acts 16:6-10) and causes him—against almost everyone's advice—to journey to Jerusalem (Acts 20:22-24). Throughout Acts, the Holy Spirit inaugurates, empowers, directs and sustains the church's mission. Through the Spirit the apostles are caught up in the Father's compassion for the world and the Son's obedience in laying himself down on its behalf. The Spirit who sheds abroad the love of God in their hearts (Romans 5:5) propels them in the overflow of that love to Jerusalem, Judea, Samaria and the ends of the earth.

In Samuel Chadwick's profound description of the church without the spirit, he states that "the Church always fails at the point of self-confidence."[17] When the church tries to send itself, to initiate and sustain the movement toward the world on its own, it always fails to overcome its inner fears and inhibitions as well as the formidable outward obstacles to mission.

As the Old Testament prophet Zechariah reminded Zerubbabel, the governor of Judah who was appointed by God to lead the returned exiles in rebuilding the temple in Jerusalem, "This is the word of the LORD to Zerubbabel: Not by might, nor by power, but by my spirit, says the LORD of hosts" (Zechariah 4:6). Zerubbabel was God's chosen leader and an extremely capable man, but God was saying, "It is not enough for you to know that I have called you to this task and given you the gifts and the talents to carry it out. Rebuilding the temple is primarily about my Spirit, not you. My Spirit himself will accomplish the work through you."

The same pattern holds true in the New Testament at the beginning of the church's life and mission. Jesus had personally chosen the apostles (the word literally means "sent ones") who were to lead the Christian movement following his resurrection and return to heaven. Moreover, he had spent three years teaching and training them. They were the God-appointed leaders and had a glorious gospel of the kingdom to proclaim. Surely then, they had all the authority, knowledge and resources necessary for the mission. But no—Jesus told them they weren't ready yet and needed to wait for the coming of the Spirit: "I am sending upon you what my Father promised; so stay here in the city until you have been clothed with power from on high" (Luke 24:49), for "you will receive power when the Holy Spirit has come upon you" (Acts 1:8). So they devoted themselves to prayer until the Day of Pentecost, when the Holy Spirit was in fact poured out (Acts 2:1-4).

Did they need the Holy Spirit so that they could obey Christ's Great Commission to make disciples of all nations? Of course. Peter's cowardice before Pentecost compared with his boldness afterward reveals the extent of their need. But if we read the story only that way, we've missed its deepest meaning. For Pentecost was not so much about the apostles' getting Holy Spirit power—like Popeye, the cartoon character, getting his can of spinach—so they could carry out the mission of Christ; rather, Pentecost was about the Holy Spirit, who is on a mission, sent by the Father and the Son, getting the apostles so that he could fulfill God's mission through them. Yes, the Spirit enabled them to go, but more important, they went because the Spirit was going. Pentecost was more about the apostles joining the Spirit than the Spirit joining them.

For those of us engaged in Christian ministry, understanding the trinitarian basis of mission is crucial because it enables us to ask the right question. Confronted with an absence of passion for mission in ourselves and others, we often ask, "What must we do to dispel our apathy and rekindle our passion for renewed mission involvement?" So we issue calls to prayer and devise strategies to motivate ourselves and others. Of course, good may come out of our efforts, but our approach is wrongheaded because it's based on the faulty assumption that mission is primarily about what we do for God.

If, however, we begin with the assumption that the Father, Son and Holy Spirit are already passionately engaged in mission to the world, the question gets reframed. Instead of "What do we have to do to stir up our passion and increase our engagement in mission?"

it becomes "What's hindering us from joining the mission in which the Father, Son and Holy Spirit are already engaged?" That's the question the rest of this chapter will wrestle with. In the process, let's consider two common barriers that hinder our participation in God's mission: our church-centered approach to ministry and our hesitancy to take risks.

FROGS OR LIZARDS?

In 1989, at the Lausanne II Congress on World Evangelization in Manila, Lee Yih, a businessman from Hong Kong, contrasted how frogs and lizards acquire food. "The frog just sits and waits and lets the food come to him. As soon as an insect gets close enough, all a frog has to do is stick out its tongue and get it. If a lizard behaved in the same way, it would soon starve. It can't afford to sit and wait. It has to go out into the world where the food can be found and hunt."[18] Yih went on to suggest that many full-time Christian workers are like frogs. They go off to Bible school or seminary, get a degree, become a pastor or join a staff at a church, and they expect that somehow the people around them will know that they are in the business of meeting spiritual needs. Soon their froglike habit of waiting for others to come to them becomes deeply ingrained.

Several years ago, guest lecturer Donna Hailson challenged the students at our seminary not to allow this to happen to them: "We can't just sit in our cozy little God boxes waiting for the world to beat a path to our doors," she insisted. "To reach the world, the Church has to break out of walls, go out of doors and lead people to the path—the narrow path that leads to life."[19] Given the increasingly post-Christian environment of North America, she challenged those whose training and experience have taught them to be ministerial frogs to become "retooled lizards."

In addition to the statue of Francis Asbury I described at the beginning of this chapter, there is another statue in the town of Wilmore that I often pass by. Directly behind our seminary library is a life-size metal statue of John Wesley—all five feet three inches of him—passionately preaching, come rain or come shine, in the open air.

Wesley's ecclesiastical context, ministerial training and personality type certainly inclined him to think and act like a ministerial frog. Ordained to the Anglican priesthood in 1728, Wesley was a strict Oxford don who was concerned that all things be done decently and in order. Preaching, therefore, should only take place indoors, behind a pulpit, within the four walls of a church sanctuary. At the time, many in the Church of England considered preaching outdoors to be a violation of civil and canonical law. As to his personal preference, Wesley would gladly have chosen the quiet of a university library or pastor's study to the noise of an unruly crowd. He was finicky about his personal appearance, always dressed as neat as a pin and wouldn't tolerate the slightest speck of dirt on his clothing.

However, ten months after his profound spiritual experience in May 1738, where his heart was "strangely warmed," the retooling process from frog to lizard began in earnest when Wesley preached in the open air for the first time. He describes his embarrassing descent into "field preaching" in his journal entry for April 2, 1739:

Mon. 2.—At four in the afternoon I submitted to be more vile and proclaimed in the highways the glad tidings of salvation speaking from a little eminence in the ground adjoining to the city to about three thousand people. The scripture on which I spoke was this, . . . "The Spirit of the Lord is upon me, because he hath anointed me to preach the gospel to the poor."[20]

Considering his church tradition and personal inclinations, the fact that he "submitted to be more vile" in such lizardlike fashion clearly indicated that Wesley had been caught up in something other than himself—God's mission—that thrust him out of his comfort zone toward lost people.

Soon he was preaching in the open air all over England. And that's what he did for the next fifty years, traveling some 225,000 miles on horseback, preaching 40,000 sermons, winning perhaps as many as 144,000 converts and establishing a vast network of Methodist societies within the Anglican Church. Yet the frog that had become a retooled lizard never became fully comfortable with field preaching. As late as 1772 he admitted, "To this day field preaching is a cross to me."[21]

By engaging in this unconventional open-air evangelism, Wesley subjected himself to criticism from family members who opposed him for what they considered an uncouth practice. His elder brother, Samuel, once wrote to their mother, Susannah, that he would rather see his brothers John and Charles "picking straws within the walls than preaching in the area of Moorfields."[22]

Anglican leaders reprimanded Wesley as well, for by engaging in field preaching across England, he was disregarding the established ecclesiastical parish boundary system. In a letter to James Harvey, who had questioned him about this, he explained why he found it necessary to invade the parishes of other clergy:

> Man forbids me do this in another's parish: that is, in effect, to do it at all; seeing I have now no parish of my own, nor probably ever shall. Whom, then, shall I hear, God or man? . . .
>
> Suffer me now to tell you my principles in this matter. I look upon all the world as my parish; thus far I mean, that in whatever part of it I am I judge it meet, right and my bounden duty

to declare, until all that are willing to hear, the glad tidings of salvation.[23]

For ministerial frogs, their parish tends to be their world. So they major on meetings, methods, maintenance and machinery rather than mission; they function more like keepers of the aquarium than fishers of men and women. But retooled ministerial lizards like Wesley, intent on participating in God's mission, view the whole world as their parish. This leads them to involve their congregation in evangelistic and social and missional work outside the walls of the church. They are determined to be witnesses, not just in Jerusalem and Judea (their immediate surroundings) but also in Samaria (across cultures) and to the ends of the earth (global).

At the end of the third and the beginning of the fourth chapter of the book of Revelation, two different types of doors are mentioned within a short span of three verses. The first is the familiar door of Revelation 3:20. Christ stands and knocks at the door of the church and the door of our heart. Here, then, is a closed door that we have to open, and in doing so, we invite Jesus to become a part of the world of our church and our life.

But then the apostle John writes, "After this I looked, and there in heaven a door stood open!" and he heard a voice beckoning, "Come up here, and I will show you what must take place after this" (Revelation 4:1). Unlike the first door, which we must open, this second door is already open, but we must enter it. And this time, instead of our inviting the Lord Jesus to become a part of *our* world, he invites us to become a part of *his* world.

In fact, from this point on in the book of Revelation, it's Christ's world that dominates. John joins in the worship of the great company around the throne in heaven; he hears the agonizing prayers of the persecuted and martyred saints; he beholds the judgments being poured out on the earth, the intensifying war in heaven and on earth, God's final victory over Satan, the establishment of God's kingdom and the final restoration of creation.

As I was thinking about these two doors, the door we open and the door we enter, it struck me that we need both doors in our ministries. Often in ministry, however, we are so preoccupied with the first—working in the church so Christ can enter—that we neglect the second—participating in Christ's larger mission in the world.

What will participating in that mission mean for you and the congregation you serve? Will it mean intentionally engaging in evangelistic and missional work outside the walls of the church sanctuary? Building short-term mission trips and opportunities for crosscultural experiences into the rhythm of church life? Becoming involved in social ministries and engaging with the poor of your community? Launching a church plant? It could mean all of these and, of course, a host of other mission strategies I haven't mentioned.

The point is, we need both doors, and we serve a parish best when we don't allow it to become our world. In fact, the more a local congregation participates in God's worldwide mission, the more its own vitality increases.

I must confess, however, that being raised in a third-generation Christian family of pastors and missionaries and graduating from a Christian college and an evangelical seminary combined to shape me into a ministerial frog more than a lizard. Consequently, for almost the first twenty years of ministry, whether I was pastoring local churches or teaching in seminary, I was focused on the door of Revelation 3:20. As the risen Christ knocked at the door of the lukewarm Laodicean church in the first century, I firmly believed he was knocking on the door of the congregations I pastored and the United

Methodist denomination I was a part of. My task, then, was to work for the renewal of the church at both congregational and denominational levels.

In 1990, however, while I was at a conference on church renewal attended by church leaders representing a wide range of American churches and denominations, I had an experience that led me through the second door of Revelation 4:1 and began my retooling from a ministerial frog to a lizard—a process that I should say is still going on. I described that experience in detail in an earlier book,[24] but let me briefly recount it here.

One evening during the conference as I lay in bed, I pictured myself standing in the United Methodist denominational vineyard in which God had called me to labor. I had been born and raised in it, my faith had been nurtured in it, my father and both my grandfathers had served it as pastors and missionaries. So I loved this vineyard and longed to see it become the kind of fruitful vineyard it was during the times of Wesley and Asbury.

Behind me I pictured the risen Christ. Since he has many vineyards in various churches and denominations, he wasn't standing in any particular vineyard. So he was outside the gate of the vineyard in which I was standing, but his presence encouraged me as I looked out across it and worked and prayed for its renewal.

Then, turning from the vineyard I had been surveying, I looked at the risen Christ. I thought he would be facing me, but to my surprise, he had his back to me. I thought he would be looking at me and my vineyard, but his tear-filled eyes were focused elsewhere—on the world beyond him. That's what he seemed most concerned about—not the renewal of my vineyard, or for that matter any of the vineyards, but the redemption of the world.

As I looked intently at the Lord Jesus, it dawned on me that if the redemption of the world is what he is most concerned about, that's what I ought to be most concerned about too. Of course, he wants to use all his vineyards toward that end, so they're all very important. He loves each of them dearly, and they're all a part of his body. But I realized that I had made the renewal of my church and denomination an end in itself. I was so intent on getting Christ into my church world (the door of Revelation 3:20) that I had failed to consider the much wider world he is so concerned about (the door of Revelation 4:1). I had invited him to come in to *my* world, but I hadn't responded to the invitation to enter *his* world.

Will my local congregation and my denomination be renewed? During almost twenty years of ministry that was the most important, pressing question for me. However, as a result of the experience I've just recounted, I'm now convinced there is a more important question: will I join Christ in his mission to the world?

For many in ministry, trained as I was to be a frog, and, after several years in ministry, comfortable and set in their froglike ways, a paradigm-shift experience may be necessary to set them on a path toward fuller engagement in God's mission and to begin the retooling process of becoming a lizard.

OUT OF OUR COMFORT ZONE

Whether such an experience is necessary or not, one thing is certain: following the triune God in mission will involve taking risks, moving out of our comfort zone, stepping out in faith toward unfamiliar places where God is leading us. Like a trapeze artist with a firm grip on the trapeze bar, we may feel comfortable and confident about the present shape and focus of our ministry. However, following God in mission often means letting go of the bar we're clutching in order to grab hold of a strange new one coming toward us.

And inevitably there is that fearful moment when we're suspended in midair. We've released our grip on the old bar, but we haven't yet grasped the new one. Someone has called this "the groan zone." It's frightening because we're out of control. We're afraid that we're going to fall and we won't make it to the next bar. So our natural inclination is to stay in our comfort zone, to cling to the bar we're currently holding. But to follow God in mission, we must be willing to risk and let go.

Peter let go when, hesitatingly, he went with the three men who had asked him to come with them to the house of Cornelius, an unkosher Gentile. God had already prepared Peter for their invitation. He had given him a vision of reptiles and animals in a sheet to teach him that "what God has made clean, you must not call profane" (Acts 10:15). Still, it was all so radical and extreme. How could a strange vision trump the established, unequivocal teaching of the Torah? Peter's precious Jewish identity, bound up with keeping the commandments, had been called into question. Yet in obedience he went, sensing that God was leading him but not knowing where he was being led.

When they arrived in Caesarea and he entered the heathen officer's house, Peter was forced out of his comfortable Jewish cocoon. That, in and of itself, was remarkable. But while he was preaching to the pagans gathered there, things really got out of hand. As missiologist Lesslie Newbigin describes it,

> Before he has finished the situation passes out of his control. Cornelius and his household are caught up, in a way that cannot be gainsaid, into the same experience of freedom and joy that Peter and the others have known since Pentecost. Peter understands that he is not in control. A power greater than his own has broken down the hedge that protects devout Jews from the uncleanness of the heathen world. Peter can do nothing but

humbly accept the fact and receive these uncircumcised pagans
by baptism into the fellowship of the church.[25]

Later, when Peter had to defend his actions before the apostles and
believers in Jerusalem, he simply recounted the amazing actions of
the Spirit and concluded, "Who was I that I could hinder God?" (Acts
11:17).

Participating with the trinitarian God in mission is like that. He is
the chief actor in the unfolding story, not us. To keep from hindering
God, we've got to risk giving up control so that he can be in control.
Often, as for Peter, it will mean that we risk looking like a fool and
that we put our religious reputation on the line.

Like Peter I have found that God is always faithful and his mission
is accomplished through me when I step out in faith and take risks.
However, often the very success engendered by taking risks for God
makes it difficult to risk again afterward. Erwin McManus is right:
"The greatest danger that success brings, aside from arrogance, is the
fear of losing what has been gained. The courage and willingness to
risk that breed success are endangered after success is obtained."[26]

So taking risks as I seek to participate in God's mission never
seems to get easier. Even though God has proved himself faithful in
the past and has blessed my steps of risky obedience, I am always
scared. I worry about the outcome and what other people will think.
It seems as if every time I let go and reach for the new trapeze bar
God is sending toward me, I have to let go of all the reputation and
security and success I've accumulated up to that point! So I always
have to overcome doubts and fears.

Yet I've found that like Indiana Jones in his desperate pursuit of
the Holy Grail, standing at the edge of a wide chasm and peering
down at the rocks below, when I lift my foot and step out into thin

air, I do not plummet to my death. Underneath are God's everlasting arms—arms that both uphold me and reach out to others to accomplish his mission through me. Someone has described their experience of risk taking like this:

> "Come to the edge," Jesus said.
> "No," I said, "I'm afraid."
> "Come to the edge," he said.
> "No," I said, "I'm afraid.
> "Come to the edge," Jesus said.
> So I came to the edge, and he pushed me.
> And together, we flew!

Indeed, participating in God's mission to the world is not a fail-safe activity. It will involve many risks with much fear and trembling. But oh, the exhilaration of soaring like an eagle, borne up by the wind of the Spirit!

And having considered them all now, these seven characteristics of trinitarian ministry—relational personhood, joyful intimacy, glad surrender, complex simplicity, gracious self-acceptance, mutual indwelling and passionate mission—how can we not also exclaim: Oh, the satisfaction of ministry in the image of God! Oh, the joy of the ministry *of* Jesus Christ, *to* the Father, *through* the Holy Spirit, for the sake of the church and the world! How can we not, like Patrick of Ireland, bind unto ourselves the strong name of the Trinity as we engage in Christian service!

Throughout our life and ministry, may we always dwell in the grace of the Lord Jesus Christ and the love of God and the fellowship of the Holy Spirit. Amen.

Notes

Chapter 1: Trinitarian Ministry

[1]Roderick Leupp, *Knowing the Name of God: A Trinitarian Tapestry of Grace, Faith and Community* (Downers Grove, Illl.: InterVarsity Press, 1996), p. 16.

[2]John Wesley, *The Works of John Wesley,* ed. Albert Outler (Nashville: Abingdon, 1985), 2:510.

[3]Henri Nouwen offers a contemplative study of Rublev's icon in his *Beholding the Beauty of the Lord* (Notre Dame, Ind.: Ave Maria, 1987), pp. 19-27. Michael Jinkins, following Nouwen, also discusses it in *Invitation to Theology* (Downers Grove, Ill.: InterVarsity Press, 2001), pp. 185-88.

[4]Nouwen, *Beholding the Beauty of the Lord,* p. 23.

[5]Ibid., pp. 20-21.

[6]Catherine Mowry LaCugna, *God for Us: The Trinity and Christian Life* (New York: HarperCollins, 1991), p. 228.

[7]Immanuel Kant, quoted in Leonardo Boff, *Trinity and Society,* trans. Paul Burns (Maryknoll, N.Y.: Orbis, 1988), p. 19.

[8]Karl Barth, *Church Dogmatics* 1/1, *The Doctrine of the Word of God,* trans. Geoffrey Bromiley (Edinburgh: T & T Clark, 1975), p. 301.

[9]David Cunningham, *These Three Are One: The Practice of Trinitarian Theology* (Oxford: Blackwell, 1998), p. 19.

[10]John R. W. Stott, *The Message of Acts* (Downers Grove, Ill.: InterVarsity Press, 1990), p. 34.

[11]I believe the Song of Solomon can and should be read on more than one level. It is a wonderful celebration of romantic human love and the beauty of sexual intimacy

in marriage. It is also an allegory of the divine-human love relationship described throughout Scripture in metaphors drawn from marriage (Isaiah 54:6; 62:5; Jeremiah 2:2; Hosea 2:19-20; John 3:29; Ephesians 5:23; Revelation 19:7; 21:2, 9; 22:17).

[12]Thomas Oden, *Pastoral Theology: Essentials for Ministry* (San Francisco: Harper & Row, 1983), p. 193.

[13]Statements like this are especially prominent in John's Gospel, where again and again Jesus stresses that the work he does is that which the Father has for him to do (cf. 5:30; 6:38; 7:18; 8:50; 9:4; 10:37-38; 12:49-50; 14:31; 15:10; 17:4).

[14]Ray Anderson, *The Shape of Practical Theology* (Downers Grove, Ill.: InterVarsity Press, 2001), p. 41.

[15]Ibid., p. 42.

[16]Oswald Chambers, *My Utmost for His Highest* (New York: Dodd, Mead, 1935), p. 277.

[17]John of the Cross, *The Collected Works of Saint John of the Cross,* trans. Kieran Kavanaugh and Otilkio Rodriguez (Washington, D.C.: ICS Publications, 1991), p. 722.

[18]See Dallas Willard, *Hearing God* (Downers Grove, Ill.: InterVarsity Press, 1999), and Gordon Smith, *Listening to God in Times of Choice* (Downers Grove, Ill.: InterVarsity Press, 1997).

[19]"The Greek and Latin Traditions Regarding the Procession of the Holy Spirit," in *Information Service of the Pontifical Council for Promoting Christian Unity,* pp. 91-92; quoted in Raniero Cantalamessa, *Come, Creator Spirit,* trans. Denis Barrett and Marlene Barrett (Collegeville, Minn.: Liturgical, 2003), pp. 375-76.

[20]Richard John Neuhaus, *Death on a Friday Afternoon* (New York: BasicBooks, 2000), p. 90.

[21]Wesley Duewel, *Ablaze for God* (Grand Rapids, Mich.: Francis Asbury, 1989), p. 78.

[22]Colin Gunton, *The Promise of the Trinity* (Edinburgh: T & T Clark, 1991), p. 37.

[23]Billy Graham, quoted in Duewel, *Ablaze for God,* pp. 308-9.

Chapter 2: Relational Personhood

[1]Larry Crabb, *Connecting: Healing for Ourselves and Our Relationships—A Radical New Vision* (Nashville: Word, 1997), p. xvi.

[2]Ibid., p. xvii.

[3]Larry Crabb, *Effective Biblical Counseling* (Grand Rapids, Mich.: Zondervan, 1977), p. 14.

[4]Boethius, quoted in Walter H. Principe, "Boethius," in *Encyclopedia of Early Christianity*, ed. Everett Ferguson (New York: Garland, 1990).

[5]Robert Bellah et al., *Habits of the Heart: Individualism and American Culture* (New York: Harper & Row, 1985), p. 142.

[6]Colin Gunton, *The Promise of the Trinity* (Edinburgh: T & T Clark, 1991), p. 10.

[7]Ibid., p. 11.

[8]See especially Stanley Grenz, *The Social God and the Relational Self* (Louisville, Ky.: Westminster John Knox, 2001).

[9]Gunton, *Promise of the Trinity*, p. 116.

[10]Michael Downey, *Altogether Gift: A Trinitarian Spirituality* (Maryknoll, N.Y.: Orbis, 2000), p. 63.

[11]Mark Shaw, *Doing Theology with Huck and Jim* (Downers Grove, Ill.: InterVarsity Press, 1993), p. 62.

[12]See Christian Schwarz, *Natural Church Development* (Carol Stream, Ill.: Church-Smart Resources, 1998).

[13]Gilbert Bilezikian, *Community 101* (Grand Rapids, Mich.: Zondervan, 1997).

[14]Stephen Stratton, "Trinity, Attachment and Love," *Catalyst* 29 (April 2003): 1-3.

[15]Ibid., p. 2.

[16]See Miroslav Volf, *Exclusion and Embrace: A Theological Exploration of Identity, Otherness and Reconciliation* (Nashville: Abingdon, 1996).

[17]John Wesley, *The Works of John Wesley* (Grand Rapids, Mich.: Zondervan, 1958), 8:272.

[18]Ibid., 8:272-73.

[19]Thomas Kelly, *A Testament of Devotion* (New York: Harper & Brothers, 1941), pp. 86-87.

[20]Salvador Minuchin, *Families and Family Therapy* (Cambridge, Mass.: Harvard University Press, 1970); *Family Kaleidoscope* (Cambridge, Mass.: Harvard University Press, 1984).

[21]Minuchin, *Family Kaleidoscope*, p. 199.

[22]Ibid., p. 91.

[23]Donald Joy, *Parents, Kids and Sexual Integrity* (Waco, Tex.: Word, 1988), p. 115.

[24]Ibid.

Chapter 3: Joyful Intimacy

[1]Jack Frost, *Experiencing the Father's Embrace* (Lake Mary, Fla.: Charisma House, 2002), pp. 4-5.

[2]Ibid., pp. 5-6.

[3]Ibid., p. 6.

[4]Ibid., p. 7.

[5]Ibid., p. 8.

[6]Ibid., pp. 9-10.

[7]Ibid., p. 10.

[8]Ibid., p. 14.

[9]Sandra Wilson, *Into Abba's Arms* (Wheaton, Ill.: Tyndale House, 1998), p. 34.

[10]Ibid., pp. 34-35.

[11]Ibid., p. 40.

[12]Wolfhart Pannenberg, *Systematic Theology,* trans. Geoffrey Bromiley (Grand Rapids: Eerdmans, 1991), 1:426.

[13]Jürgen Moltmann, *The Trinity and the Kingdom,* trans. Margaret Kohl (San Francisco: Harper & Row, 1981), p. 59.

[14]Leanne Payne, *Real Presence* (Grand Rapids, Mich.: Baker, 1995), p. 81.

[15]Jon Tal Murphree, *The Trinity and Human Personality* (Nappanee, Ind.: Evangel, 2001), p. 29.

[16]See Leon Morris, *The Gospel According to John* (Grand Rapids: Eerdmans, 1971), p. 76.

[17]Roderick Leupp, *Knowing the Name of God* (Downers Grove, Ill.: InterVarsity Press, 1996), p. 162.

[18]See Jean Galot, *Abba Father: We Long to See Your Face,* trans. M. Angeline Bouchard (New York: Alba House, 1992), p. 58.

[19]John of the Cross, quoted in Paul Fiddes, *Participating in God* (Louisville, Ky.: Westminster John Knox Press, 2000), p. 45.

[20]Clark Pinnock, *Flame of Love* (Downers Grove, Ill.: InterVarsity Press, 1996), p. 39.

[21]James D. G. Dunn, *Romans 1-8,* Word Biblical Commentary 38A (Dallas: Word, 1988), p. 462.

[22]Henri J. M. Nouwen, *Here and Now* (New York: Crossroad, 1995), p. 100.

[23]Frank Lake, *Clinical Theology* (London: Darton, Longman & Todd, 1966), p. 135.

[24]Ibid.

[25]Mike Bickle, *The Pleasures of Loving God* (Lake Mary, Fla.: Creation House, 2000), p. 47.

[26]From a newsletter Tammy Hutchins sent to her friends and supporters, August 1997.

[27]Craig Keener, *Gift and Giver: The Holy Spirit for Today* (Grand Rapids: Baker, 2001), p. 18.

[28]Ibid.

[29]Brennan Manning, *Abba's Child* (Colorado Springs: NavPress, 1994), p. 51.

[30]Charles Stanley, "Emotional Baggage in Ministry," *Christian Counseling Today,* January 1993, p. 35.

[31]For more on bringing our hurts to the cross, see Stephen Seamands, *Wounds That Heal* (Downers Grove, Ill.: InterVarsity Press, 2003).

[32]J. Sidlow Baxter, *Awake, My Heart* (Grand Rapids: Kregel, 1994), p. 24.

[33]Andrew Murray, *Abide in Christ* (Old Tappan, N.J.: Fleming H. Revell, n.d.), pp. 124-25.

[34]Ibid., p. 125.

[35]John Wesley, *The Works of John Wesley,* vol. 7, *A Collection of Hymns for the Use of the People Called Methodists,* ed. Franz Hildebrandt and Oliver A. Beckerlegge (Nashville: Abingdon, 1983), pp. 258-59.

Chapter 4: Glad Surrender

[1]Hannah Hurnard, *Hinds' Feet on High Places* (Uhrichsville, Ohio: Barbour, 1977), p. 60.

[2]Ibid., p. 184.

[3]Ibid., p. 186.

[4]Ibid.

[5]Ibid., p. 187.

[6]Ibid., p. 254.

[7]Roderick Leupp, *Knowing the Name of God* (Downers Grove, Ill.: InterVarsity Press, 1996), p. 28.

[8]Jürgen Moltmann, *The Trinity and the Kingdom,* trans. Margaret Kohl (San Francisco: Harper & Row, 1981), p. 83.

[9]Rowan Williams, quoted in Miroslav Volf, *Exclusion and Embrace: A Theological Exploration of Identity, Otherness and Reconciliation* (Nashville: Abingdon, 1996), p. 127.

[10]Henri J. M. Nouwen, *Behold the Beauty of the Lord: Praying with Icons* (Notre Dame, Ind.: Ave Maria, 1987), p. 25.

[11]Ibid.

[12]Geoffrey Wainright, *Doxology: The Praise of God in Worship, Doctrine and Life* (New York: Oxford University Press, 1980), p. 23.

[13]Wolfhart Pannenberg, *Systematic Theology,* trans. Geoffrey Bromiley (Grand Rapids: Eerdmans, 1991), 1:308-13.

[14]Colin Gunton, *The Promise of the Trinity* (Edinburgh: T & T Clark, 1991), p. 174.

[15]C. S. Lewis, *The Problem of Pain* (New York: Macmillan, 1962), p. 152.

[16]Richard John Neuhaus, *Death on a Friday Afternoon* (New York: BasicBooks, 2000), p. 134.

[17]John R. W. Stott, *The Cross of Christ* (Downers Grove, Ill.: InterVarsity Press, 1986), p. 322.

[18]There is disagreement among scholars as to whether in Romans 7 Paul is describing the struggle of a regenerate Christian or an unregenerate person striving to obey the law. Personally I believe it is the unregenerate person. But regardless of whom Paul has in mind, I believe that what Paul says resonates with the actual experience of both types of persons.

[19]C. S. Lewis, *Mere Christianity* (New York: Macmillan, 1960).

[20]Ibid., p. 167.

[21]Mike Breaux shared this in a sermon he preached at Asbury Theological Seminary's Ministry Conference, February 4, 2004.

[22]George Müller, quoted in W. E. Sangster, *The Pure in Heart* (London: Epworth, 1954), p. 141.

[23]Thomas Kelly, *A Testament of Devotion* (New York: Harper & Brothers, 1941), p. 52.

[24]Hurnard, *Hinds' Feet,* p. 60.

[25]George Matheson, "Make Me a Captive, Lord," 1890.

[26]Henry Blackaby and Richard Blackaby, *Spiritual Leadership* (Nashville: Broadman & Holman, 2001), p. 70.

[27]Oswald Chambers, *My Utmost for His Highest* (New York: Dodd, Mead, 1935), p. 18.

Chapter 5: Complex Simplicity

[1]Thomas Oden, *The Living God* (San Francisco: Harper & Row, 1987), p. 217.

[2]Augustine, quoted in Roger Olson and Christopher Hall, *The Trinity* (Grand Rapids: Eerdmans, 2002), p. 49.

[3]C. S. Lewis, *Mere Christianity* (New York: Macmillan, 1960), pp. 141-42.

[4]Gregory Nazianzen, quoted in Oden, *Living God,* p. 216.

[5]Gerhard Tersteegen, quoted in D. M. Baillie, *Out of Nazareth* (New York: Charles Scribner's Sons, 1958), p. 71.

[6]Oden, *Living God,* p. 215.

[7]*The Catechism of the Catholic Church,* quoted in Michael Downey, *Altogether Gift: A Trinitarian Spirituality* (Maryknoll, N.Y.: Orbis, 2000), p. 40.

[8]A. W. Tozer, *The Knowledge of the Holy* (New York: Harper & Row, 1961), p. 33.

[9]Ignaz Franz, "Holy God, We Praise Thy Name," in *The United Methodist Hymnal* (Nashville: United Methodist Publishing House, 1989), p. 79.

[10]Augustine, quoted in Roderick Leupp, *Knowing the Name of God* (Downers Grove, Ill.: InterVarsity Press, 1996), p. 172.

[11]Karl Rahner, *The Trinity* (New York: Herder & Herder, 1970), p. 50.

[12]Eugene Peterson and Marva Dawn, *The Unnecessary Pastor* (Grand Rapids: Eerdmans, 2000), p. 68.

[13]Ibid., p. 69.

[14]D. M. Baillie, *God Was in Christ* (New York: Charles Scribner's Sons, 1948), p. 109.

[15]Gordon Fee, *Paul, the Spirit and the People of God* (Peabody, Mass.: Hendrickson, 1996), p. 146.

[16]Christian Schwarz, *Paradigm Shift in the Church* (Carol Stream, Ill.: ChurchSmart Resources, 1999), p. 7.

[17]Ibid., p. 16.

[18]Ibid., p. 22.

[19]Ibid., p. 214.

[20]Ibid., pp. 215-16.

[21]Leonard Hodgson, *The Doctrine of the Trinity* (New York: Charles Scribner's Sons, 1944), p. 90.

[22]Clark Pinnock, *Flame of Love* (Downers Grove, Ill.: InterVarsity Press, 1996), p. 29.

[23]Ken Blue, *Authority to Heal* (Downers Grove, Ill.: InterVarsity Press, 1987). See especially pp. 41-51, 97-105.

[24]Alfred North Whitehead, quoted in Richard John Neuhaus, *Death on a Friday Afternoon* (New York: BasicBooks, 2000), p. 5.

[25]David Hansen, *The Art of Pastoring* (Downers Grove, Ill.: InterVarsity Press, 1994), p. 9.

[26]Ibid., p. 10.

[27]Neuhaus, *Death on a Friday Afternoon,* p. 217.

[28]Ibid., pp. 217-18.

Chapter 6: Gracious Self-Acceptance

[1]John Zizoulas, quoted in Colin Gunton, *The Promise of the Trinity* (Edinburgh: T & T Clark, 1991), p. 97.

[2]John of Damascus, quoted in Thomas Oden, *The Living God* (San Francisco: Harper & Row, 1987), p. 218.

[3]David Cunningham, *These Three Are One* (Oxford: Blackwell, 1998), p. 117.

[4]Ibid., p. 198.

[5]Richard John Neuhaus, *Death on a Friday Afternoon* (New York: BasicBooks, 2000), p. 131.

[6]William Wordsworth, quoted in Jon Tal Murphree, *The Trinity and Human Personality* (Nappanee, Ind.: Evangel, 2001), p. 58.

[7]Colin Gunton, *Father, Son and Holy Spirit* (London: T & T Clark, 2003), p. 15.

[8]Colin Gunton, *The One, the Three and the Many* (Cambridge: Cambridge University Press, 1993), p. 196.

[9]G. K. Chesterton, quoted in Thomas Dubay, *The Evidential Power of Beauty* (San Francisco: Ignatius, 1999), p. 176.

[10]Catherine Mowry LaCugna, *God for Us* (San Francisco: HarperCollins, 1991), p. 299.

[11]Lamin Sanneh, *Whose Religion Is Christianity?* (Grand Rapids: Eerdmans, 2003), p. 106.

[12]Ibid., pp. 99-100.

[13]Ibid., p. 100.

[14]Michael Ramsey, quoted in Steve Harper, "The Power of One Life," *Asbury Herald* 113 (Spring/Summer 2003): 3-4.

[15]C. G. Jung, *Modern Man in Search of a Soul* (New York: Harcourt, Brace & World, 1933), p. 235.

[16]Brennan Manning, *A Glimpse of Jesus* (San Francisco: HarperCollins, 2003) p. ix.

[17]Henri J. M. Nouwen, *Life of the Beloved* (New York: Crossroad, 1992), p. 21.

[18]David Seamands, *Healing for Damaged Emotions* (Wheaton, Ill.: Victor, 1981), pp. 48-56.

[19]Romano Guardini, quoted in Leanne Payne, *Restoring the Christian Soul Through Healing Prayer* (Wheaton, Ill.: Crossway, 1991), p. 31.

[20]Ibid., p. 32.

[21]Simon Tugwell, quoted in Brennan Manning, *Abba's Child* (Colorado Springs, Colo.: NavPress, 1994), p. 18.

[22]Ibid., pp. 21-22.

[23]C. S. Lewis, *Mere Christianity* (New York: Macmillan, 1960), p. 190.

[24]John Eagan, *A Traveler Toward the Dawn* (Chicago: Loyola University Press, 1990), p. xii.

[25]Ibid., p. 150.

[26]George Bernanos, *The Diary of a Country Priest* (New York: Sheed & Ward, 1936), p. 178.

Chapter 7: Mutual Indwelling

[1]Peter Xu Yongze, quoted in Paul Hattaway, *Back to Jerusalem* (Waynesboro, Ga.: Gabriel, 2003), p. 6.

[2]Hudson Taylor, quoted in Howard Taylor and Geraldine Taylor, *Hudson Taylor's Spiritual Secret* (Chicago: Moody Press, n.d.), p. 153.

[3]Ibid., p. 156.

[4]Ibid., pp. 161-63.

[5]Council of Florence, quoted in Randall E. Otto, "The Use and Abuse of Perichoresis in Recent Theology," *Scottish Journal of Theology* 54 (2001): 372.

[6]David Cunningham, *These Three Are One* (Malden, Mass.: Blackwell, 1998), pp. 178-79.

[7]Jürgen Moltmann, *The Trinity and the Kingdom* (San Francisco: Harper & Row, 1981), p. 175.

[8]John of Damascus, quoted in Timothy George, *Is the Father of Jesus the God of Muhammed?* (Grand Rapids: Zondervan, 2002), pp. 85-86.

[9]Peter Drilling, *Trinity and Ministry* (Minneapolis: Fortress, 1991), pp. 34-35.

[10]Paul Fiddes, *Participating in God* (Louisville, Ky.: Westminster John Knox, 2000), p. 72.

[11]Catherine Mowry LaCugna, *God for Us* (San Francisco: HarperCollins, 1991), p. 272.

[12]Leonide Ouspensky and Vladimir Lossky, *The Meaning of Icons* (Crestwood, N.Y.: St. Vladimir's Seminary Press, 1982), p. 202.

[13]Miroslav Volf, *After Our Likeness* (Grand Rapids: Eerdmans, 1998), p. 211.

[14]Ruth Paxson, *Life on the Highest Plane* (Chicago: Moody Press, 1928), 2:91.

[15]See the discussion of this in Michael J. Gorman, *Cruciformity: Paul's Narrative Spirituality of the Cross* (Grand Rapids: Eerdmans, 2001), pp. 35-49.

[16]Adolf Deissmann, quoted in ibid., p. 38.

[17]Richard B. Hays, *The Faith of Jesus Christ: An Investigation of the Narrative Substructure of Galatians 3:1-4:11,* SBLDS 56 (Chico, Calif.: Scholars, 1983), p. 168.

[18]Sadu Sundar Singh, quoted in Nick Harrison, ed., *His Victorious Indwelling* (Grand Rapids: Zondervan, 1998), p. 108.

[19]Stephen Olford, *The Way of Holiness* (Wheaton, Ill.: Crossway, 1998), p. 59.

[20]Cunningham, *These Three Are One,* p. 165.

[21]R. Paul Stevens, *The Other Six Days* (Grand Rapids: Eerdmans, 1999), p. 62.

[22]Dietrich Bonhoeffer, *Life Together* (New York: Harper & Row, 1954), pp. 97, 99.

[23]Michael Nichols, *The Lost Art of Listening* (New York: Guilford, 1995), p. 62.

[24]Ibid., p. 15.

[25]Fiddes, *Participating in God,* p. 123.

[26]Amy Carmichael, *The Gold Cord* (New York: Macmillan, 1932), p. 31.

[27]Ajith Fernando, *Jesus Driven Ministry* (Wheaton, Ill.: Crossway, 2002), p. 131.

[28]George Cladis, *Leading the Team-Based Church* (San Francisco: Jossey-Bass, 1999), p. 4.

[29]Michael Jinkins, *Invitation to Theology* (Downers Grove, Ill.: InterVarsity Press, 2001), p. 93.

[30]Mike Mason, *The Mystery of Marriage* (Portland, Ore.: Multnomah Press, 1985), pp. 34-35.

Chapter 8: Passionate Mission

[1]Francis Asbury, *The Journal and Letters of Francis Asbury,* ed. Elmer T. Clark, J. Manning Potts and Jacob S. Payton (Nashville: Abingdon, 1958), 1:422-23.

[2]Darius Salter, *America's Bishop: The Life of Francis Asbury* (Nappanee, Ind.: Francis Asbury, 2003), p. 110.

[3]Ibid., p. 115.

[4]International Missionary Council of 1952, quoted in R. Paul Stevens, *The Other Six Days* (Grand Rapids, Mich.: Eerdmans, 2000), p. 193.

[5]Stevens, *Other Six Days,* p. 194.

[6]Jürgen Moltmann, *The Church in the Power of the Spirit,* trans. Margaret Kohl (San Francisco: Harper & Row, 1977), p. 64.

[7]Ibid., pp. 53-56. See also Jürgen Moltmann, *The Trinity and the Kingdom,* trans. Margaret Kohl (San Francisco: Harper & Row, 1981), pp. 65-75.

[8]C. S. Lewis, *Mere Christianity* (New York: Macmillan, 1960), p. 151.

[9]Ibid., p. 152.

[10]Jonathan Edwards, quoted in Daniel Migliore, *Faith Seeking Understanding* (Grand Rapids: Eerdmans, 1991), p. 85.

[11]Moltmann, *Trinity and the Kingdom,* p. 58.

[12]Moltmann, *Church in the Power of the Spirit,* pp. 55-56.

[13]David Bosch, *Transforming Mission* (Maryknoll, N.Y.: Orbis, 1991), p. 390.

[14]Leonard Sweet, *A Cup of Coffee at the Soul Café* (Nashville: Broadman, 1998), p. 29-30.

[15]Oswald Chambers, *So Send I You* (Bristol, U.K.: Marshall Morgan & Scott, 1988), p. 161.

[16]Lewis, *Mere Christianity,* p. 153.

[17]Samuel Chadwick, *The Way to Pentecost* (Fort Washington, Penn.: Christian Literature Crusade, 1969), p. 15.

[18]Lee Yih, quoted in Donna F. G. Hailson, "Retooled Lizards within the Contemporary 'Navigational Environment,'" *Asbury Herald* 112 (Winter/Spring 2000): 7.

[19]Ibid., p. 8.

[20]John Wesley, *The Works of John Wesley* (Grand Rapids: Zondervan, 1958), 1:185.

[21]Ibid., 3:479.

[22]Samuel Wesley, quoted in A. Skevington Wood, *The Burning Heart* (Grand Rapids, Mich.: Eerdmans, 1967), p. 95.

[23]John Wesley, *The Letters of John Wesley,* ed. John Telford (London: Epworth, 1931), 1:286.

[24]Stephen Seamands, *Holiness of Heart and Life* (Nashville: Abingdon, 1990), p. 93-95.

[25]Lesslie Newbigin, *The Open Secret* (Grand Rapids: Eerdmans, 1995), p. 59.

[26]Erwin McManus, *Seizing Your Divine Moment* (Nashville: Thomas Nelson, 2002), p. 39.